The Lord Gave Me This

The Lord Gave Me This

Understanding Historic Leadership
Development Practices of the Black Church
to Prepare Tomorrow's Leaders

TERRELL CARTER

WIPF *&* STOCK · Eugene, Oregon

THE LORD GAVE ME THIS
Understanding Historic Leadership Development Practices of the Black
Church to Prepare Tomorrow's Leaders

Wipf & Stock
An Imprint of Wipf and Stock Publishers
199 W. 8th Ave., Suite 3
Eugene, OR 97401

www.wipfandstock.com

PAPERBACK ISBN: 978-1-4982-3938-7
HARDCOVER ISBN: 978-1-4982-3940-0
EBOOK ISBN: 978-1-4982-3939-4

Manufactured in the U.S.A.   09/19/16

This book is dedicated to the many people who supported me throughout the process of completing it.

To Drs. Ircel Harrison, C. Jeff Woods, Bob Harris, and Rev. Jimi Gwynn. Thanks for challenging and encouraging me to pursue this project. I hope to be as faithful a mentor to others as you all have been to me.

To the Carter clan for continual love and patience.

To Genevieve and Jerry Carter for life more abundantly.

Contents

Illustrations and Tables

Chapter One

What's the Point of This Book?

THE PURPOSE OF THIS book has been to discover the most effective ministry development training practices to help African American church leaders and pastors become more effective leaders within the contexts they serve. This book investigates a variety of ministry development training processes through critical research, individual and group interviews, and both formal and informal discussion groups in order to discover which process is most effective in preparing tomorrow's leaders. The first step in answering this question is to understand the training practices of leaders of the early church and then compare them with the current practices traditionally employed within the African American context.

WHAT IS THE NEW TESTAMENT MODEL FOR LEADERSHIP DEVELOPMENT?

The best manual we have to guide our thoughts on church leadership development is the word of Jesus as found in the gospels, as well as the words of his apostles as found in a handful of epistles in the New Testament, primarily 1 and 2 Timothy and Titus. The practices we find in these letters give us a solid foundation to work with as we seek to understand God's desires for leadership development.

Upon a general review of these books, it seems that God's desire is for leadership development to be managed through the church:

> The ideals of the core principles found in the letters to the first churches [especially Ephesians] and to church leaders [Timothy and Titus] point to the biblical nature of leadership training being church-based. Training took place in the context of the ministry. Training was viewed as an entrusting of the ministry to faithful men by faithful men who were doing the work of the ministry. Confirming of those trained was fundamentally the responsibility of leaders at a local church level.[1]

Within the epistles to Timothy and Titus, Paul commands leaders to live their lives as examples for others to follow, to live out their faith through their relationships with their family members, to study God's word in-depth and be able to defend the church's teachings, to fight against false and heretical teachings, to cast out false teachers, to mentor others within their congregations, to live in peace with each other as much as humanly possible, and to even separate themselves from people who are not following the established doctrines of the church.

Outside of these commands, there are no other strict set of criteria laid out in the New Testament for how a church leader is to be trained. This leaves the process of leadership training open to the creative impulses of those who are leading the training process, as "the church-based training of the Early Church was clearly understood as a flexible leadership development strategy rooted in the life and ministry of local churches, in which gifted men entrusted more and more of the ministry to other faithful men while they themselves remained deeply involved in the process of establishing churches."[2]

---

1. Reed, "Church-Based Theological Education," 8.
2. Ibid.

With this flexibility in mind, I will briefly explore a few initial differences in how this flexibility has played out in the leadership development processes within black and white contexts.

SOME INITIAL DIFFERENCES BETWEEN BLACKS AND WHITES AS THEY RELATE TO MINISTRY LEADERSHIP DEVELOPMENT

For multiple historic reasons that I will highlight shortly, on the whole, African Americans are far less likely than their white counterparts to obtain higher levels of education past the high school level: "African American Protestants tend to have lower levels of educational attainment than the general population. Eighteen percent of black Protestants have a college degree, compared to 27% of the general population. A majority of black Protestants (57%) have a high school education or less, compared to half the general population."[3]

Conversely, within the black church, leadership development has little to do with participation in a certain educational program. Instead, it depends more on whether God has "called" a person to ministerial service within the church context and whether that person is able to prove this calling through preaching and serving the church immediately.

> Foundational to understanding this issue is the reality that within the African-American community the whole issue of call and access to ministry is totally contrary to what is typically observed in white settings. For example, an African-American comes to know Christ, senses God's call to minister, acknowledges that call before others through what is known as a "trial sermon," becomes ordained, enters ministry, and then somewhere down the line might go back to school in order to receive some type of formal theological training.[4]

3. Laser, "Beyond the God Gap," 29.
4. Fuder, *Heart for the City*, 2543–552.

This is essentially the antithesis of the training tract found within white contexts. "The process of ministry accessibility is totally opposite in most situations in the white community. Here, a person senses God's call, goes off to seminary or Bible college, and then, after graduating from seminary or Bible college, gets ordained and moves into full-time vocational ministry."[5]

Another reason for the divergent views between the ethnicities is that the environments cultivated at white seminaries are not always welcoming to African American students. "Part of the reason for this abysmal showing [of black students at white seminaries] is the perception by some who have attended such schools that not only are they not user-friendly environments, but that they are downright 'hostile,' in a covert way, to African-Americans who choose to attend."[6]

The reasons for this highlight the perception that white instructors and curriculum developers operate from a position of power over minorities:

> There are a number of reasons for this perception, ranging from the subtle inferences of a curriculum that looks at the history of the church and lists primarily European and/or European-Americans as significant contributors, to the area of systematic theology that uses terminology such as "black" to represent evil and "white" to represent good. In addition, practical theology communicates, either outwardly or by implication, the perception that some of the cultural expressions of African-American faith are incorrect because they do not line up with the expectations of the majority community. The lack of minority faculty as role models and administrators also contributes to this perception of an unfriendly, if not hostile environment.[7]

As long as this perception persists, black students will likely continue to be hesitant to enter traditional educational programs

5. Ibid.
6. Ibid., 2636–641.
7. Ibid.

that they assume will not benefit them or the unique needs of their individual congregations. Indeed, "It is not logical to assume that a curriculum geared largely to the expectations of white, middle-class Protestantism will produce competent leadership for churches that are urban, frequently located in or near ghettos, and with poor and insecure constituencies."[8]

In order to better understand this divide, I will briefly review how the educational practices for leadership development have historically differed between the races.

8. Rooks, "Crisis in Church Negro Leadership," 328–29.

Chapter Two

A Brief Comparison of Leadership Training Practices in White and Black Contexts

A BRIEF SURVEY OF HISTORIC WHITE THEOLOGICAL EDUCATIONAL MODELS

SOME SCHOLARS WOULD ARGUE that since our nation's founding, education has been for the benefit of a special class of people that did not include blacks:

> By the early nineteenth century, there existed a small group of colleges whose students consisted mostly of the sons of the wealthiest and most elite families in the colonies, as well as a few young male students of high promise from middle and lower income families. Most of the latter received scholarships, which they combined with work to pay for their tuition. All of these students were being educated to assume a leadership role in society, and were expected to be gentlemen who were religious, articulate, and analytical. The new nation now had a new system of higher education that was exclusively for the benefit of white males. No blacks or women needed to apply because none would be admitted.[1]

1. Farley, *Theologia*, 5.

For the most part, this expectation that white leaders would obtain a certain level of education rang true within the white church context as well. Leaders were expected to be educated and competent in order to fulfill their ministerial responsibilities. "From the founding of the first colonies to the rise of the first seminaries, the congregations expected the minister to be educated."[2] The process of education for these leaders was expected to occur through some formal setting. That is, "even if only a certain percentage of ministers completed the college degree, it was assumed that the education of the minister occurred at a school."[3]

Within the context of attending a formal school, pastoral leaders were expected to study multiple higher-level subjects. "The basis of education was thorough grounding in biblical and classical languages, and the education in divinity was primarily the study of Scripture and the guides, handbooks, or compendia of dogmatics and ethics being written by continental and English theologians."[4] This first degree would not be the end of the formal educational process. "In this period the first step was taken to distinguish ministerial education from college education, the practice of doing 'graduate study' in the subject of divinity. Thus many returned to the college for a special two-year course in divinity."[5]

Over time, the process of education shifted from primarily occurring within classrooms to practical apprenticeships with active pastors:

> In the mid-eighteenth century there arose the practice of seeking education in divinity with a pastor who was willing to accept one or more students. Modeled on an English practice, these schools of the prophets answered to a new population of believers and clergy created by the Great Awakening. In many cases this too was "graduate education," in that ministers with college degrees

2. Ibid., 6.
3. Ibid.
4. Ibid., 7.
5. Ibid.

sought further work in divinity with a well-known pastor-teacher.[6]

The point of this shift was to allow ministers to gain practical experience that augmented their book-based knowledge through a mentoring relationship with a qualified pastor. Eventually, the process of educating white congregational leaders became anchored within the context of seminaries, which required students to move from their homes in order to live on campus and share the learning experience with other students within a controlled environment. In fact, "in the decades preceding the Civil War, the center of theological education moved from parsonage seminaries or log colleges, which required college or an equivalent education followed by divinity study under the tutelage of a minister, to formal theological institutions called seminaries, which required an in-residence training as preparation for future service."[7]

The primary reasons for this were to

- allow sufficient time to study;
- provide access to a suitable library;
- promote the ability to pursue an area of specialized study;
- allow greater devotion of time to study and teaching;
- allow students to profit from other ministerial candidates by forming friendships that promote harmony in the church; and
- promote unity and one-mindedness in the church by teaching ministerial students sound doctrine in one institution.[8]

These are all worthwhile reasons to engage in the seminary process. One of the problems was that African Americans were not afforded the same types of opportunities.

6. Ibid.
7. Reed, "Church-Based Theological Education," 3.
8. Ibid., 4.

A BRIEF SURVEY OF THEOLOGICAL EDUCATION WITHIN THE BLACK CHURCH EXPERIENCE

It is no secret that the educational opportunities and environments for study that were readily available for white church leaders were not available for African American ministers. Historically, educational opportunities for African Americans were often no more than a dream: "Education was not readily available to African Americans who were kept in bondage in slavery—regardless how much they might have wanted to learn."[9]

When educational opportunities were available for blacks, those institutions often did not offer programming that legitimately sought to educate those who attended. Indeed, "when looking at the founding of colleges in the United States, it is apparent that blacks and women were not included. In order to remedy this situation, black colleges and women's colleges sprang up, but they were of an inferior quality."[10]

Since the traditional means of education that were available to white pastors were not available to their black counterparts, the black church had to be creative in its process of preparing its ministers for leadership: "The process of religious education has indicated that non-traditional forms of education are the ones primarily at play in the Black Church. The homiletic language, often emerging through preaching, and the therapeutic language, as demonstrated in spirituals and storytelling, are valid and widely observed methods of religious education."[11]

This process of preparing leaders through the practice of preaching and storytelling—instead of through structured learning in a classroom setting—was a respected process that had been handed down for generations. "Coming from an oral culture in Africa, it was common for the young people to learn by listening to the stories and conversations of the griots in their midst. Therefore,

---

9. Etindi, "Training Ministers," 19.

10. Bradley, *Aliens in the Promised Land*, 108.

11. Hinton, *Commercial Church*, 24.

it was natural even here in America for those 'called to preach' to learn by example to follow in the steps of their predecessors."[12]

After reaching the United States and experiencing a violent world of racial segregation, this practice was continued by Africans and their descendants out of necessity:

> When Black preachers in the South were forbidden to teach others to read or write they could only train other ministers by helping them memorize Scripture, illustrating how to preach, and demonstrating how to perform whatever sacraments were a part of their faith tradition. Often these things were done covertly to avoid the legal or de facto consequences for such practices. There was nothing unusual or substandard about such apprenticeships in that day. That pattern was part of everyday life in an oral culture.[13]

Because of the circumstances in which they found themselves, African Americans typically belonged to a close-knit community. Because of this closeness, the idea of someone leaving their community in order to be trained to serve the community was a foreign idea. "Given the critical importance of community among African Americans and within the Black church itself, how very foreign it would be for a local church to simply send away those from their community who are called into vocational ministry in order for them to be educated and trained entirely outside of that community."[14]

Instead of leaving the community, black church leaders were expected to live among the people that they served, learn the needs of those people, and develop the means to help them with the daily challenges that they faced:

> Because African American churches have historically been involved in addressing the unique social challenges that affect Black populations, African American clergy have often assumed roles outside those traditionally

12. Etindi, "Training Ministers," 14.

13. Ibid.

14. Ibid., 10.

associated with pastoral responsibilities. In addition to the roles of preacher, counselor, and director of religious life, African American clergy have also had to assume the roles of activists, grassroots organizers, economic developers, and community advocates.[15]

Due to the unique role of the black pastors within the community, their educational needs will tend to vary greatly from those of their white counterparts, centering more on the social and economic needs of church members instead of strict doctrinal concerns. That is, "by virtue of this group's leadership of religious bodies with a historical legacy of working on issues of social justice, political enfranchisement, and economic empowerment, the professional development of the African American clergy can be correlated to quality-of-life issues in the communities which they serve."[16]

CONCERNS OF THE BLACK CHURCH WITH TRADITIONAL WHITE THEOLOGICAL EDUCATION

In addition to the aforementioned concerns held by African American ministers and congregations, there is another concern that is built less on academic fidelity and more on a person's ability to communicate the faith like those from prior generations:

> Perhaps of greater consequence for the black church is the implicit antagonism toward intellectual zeal sometimes found within the church walls. Certainly, no one openly speaks against formal theology or critical reflection in church. However, there is an implicit antagonism that can be at play. The nearly uniform rejection of the intellectual elite has historically meant that everyone has received the same level and quality of religious instruction in the black church. While this does ensure some

15. Colvin, "Examination of the Professional Development," 2.
16. Ibid.

equity, it works against advancing the level and quality of religious education.[17]

The reason for this antagonism is because, historically, the black church is less concerned with educational credentials and more concerned with a persons' ability to preach in a way that connects with listeners: "The question for the Black preacher, historically, has not been where they graduated from or what seminary they were connected to, or even what fraternity; the question is 'can they tell the story?'"[18]

This ability to "tell the story"—that is, to preach—is the standard by which most leaders are judged successful (or not) by those they serve. This unwritten measurement of effectiveness has led to the perception that church leaders do not need to achieve a certain level of education if they can preach in such a way that those they serve feel they have been touched by their preaching.

This ability to preach also reflects the validity of receiving a "call to ministry" from God:

> The concept of the call of God and the bond of trust between the minister and the community, have created an ongoing controversy regarding education that is not true among candidates for other professions. No one questions that someone wanting to be a doctor should go to college and medical school; no one questions that someone wanting to be a lawyer should go to college and law school. But the level and type of education needed for one who "is called" into ministry has continued to this day to be held in question—granted, in some circles more than others.[19]

Pastors Derek Prime and Alistair Begg have given an adequate explanation of what it means to be "called" in the black church context. They say, "By call we mean the unmistakable conviction an individual possesses that God wants him to do a specific

17. Hinton, *Commercial Church*, 37.
18. Johnson, "Theological Pathways," 10.
19. Etindi, "Training Ministers," 19.

task."[20] Typically, that call includes some type of preaching and public leadership responsibility. This calling to ministry differs from white traditions that allow for a person to experience a call from God as well as for the idea that if a person wants to serve in ministry, they are free to pursue that personal desire. Many black churches would consider this kind of process presumptuous and not led by the Spirit of God.

One of the downfalls of this type of calling is that simply hearing from God is the primary prerequisite for a person that wants to preach in an organized church context. According to Charles V. Hamilton, a political scientist and former Columbia University professor, one "phenomenon operating against strong emphasis on formal training has been the 'call to the ministry.' A man who is called is one chosen and prepared by God for the responsibilities of being a good preacher."[21]

It is naturally assumed that if God has called someone, then God will equip that person for the task ahead:

> "God equips the called" is a common refrain. To some, that means a supernatural equipping—an act of the Holy Spirit anointing the individual and gifting him/her to preach. Other than acknowledging a necessity to "know that Bible," any other preparation (i.e., "equipping") seems superfluous to those of that mindset. As Daniel concluded in his study, "the 'call-to-the-ministry' belief, to which the students have been accustomed in their home communities, and which is held by most of the ministerial students, tends to minimize the importance of a high-grade theological education, and to discount its value."[22]

In addition to a calling to the ministry that carries more weight than any academic program of leadership preparation, black leaders are also concerned with the opinions of the people they plan to serve through the church. As a result, "another factor

20. Ibid., 48.
21. Ibid., 22.
22. Ibid.

that has not helped to encourage formal education among ministers is the attitude voiced by some people in the minister's own churches—those communities that continue to have great influence in their lives."[23]

In the black church, understanding the people that you will serve is more important than understanding Greek or obscure theological definitions. "The first lesson [learned] was that if you're going to pastor black people, you'd damn well better throw away the books you learned from in seminary and look at the people you're dealing with."[24]

Within the black church, instead of being a point of celebration, obtaining a certain level of academic achievement can actually count against a leader. As Reverend Henry Lewis, a professor and chaplain at Winston-Salem State University, has noted, "Many of our people. . . have been oriented around the idea that if the minister is called, then all this education we're getting isn't necessary. God will give you what you need. And with this education, you get over your heads. You come with an educated sermon, and nobody understands you."[25]

The reason for this attitude is based partly on the belief that any education and leadership development that positively impacts the black community occurs through active daily participation within that community and not through separation at a college campus:

> Good leaders are those who faithfully embody the basic traditions and values of those who are being led, and who have the ability to inspire the loyalty of the latter. As implied previously, the development of good leaders requires a communal context, wherein teachers are exemplars of the desired goal, and wherein the willing association between teachers and students engages all in the process of constructing a common life through common work, study, recreation, and worship. Traditionally,

23. Ibid., 24.
24. Ibid., 25.
25. Ibid.

the black churches have been the loci for the development of this type of community.[26]

This process of learning and leading in practical areas, especially preaching, together with the ability to have those skills verified by another congregation, typically carries more weight for a potential clergy person than having earned a particular degree.

> Another major struggle that hinders the appreciation of theological training for clergy in the African American Baptist church is within our structure and polity. As Baptists, we are autonomous and congregational. . .Because of this autonomy, there is no universal standard of theological training. Many churches who are in search of a pastor will ask that the applicant present some form of theological training or education; but countless non-credentialed clergy are called to Baptist churches every year on their preaching ability and previous pastoral experience alone."[27]

With the knowledge that they can become pastors even without earning a degree, fledgling leaders may not be adequately motivated to seek formal education. When added to the fact that multiple leaders are successfully called to lead congregations with minimal personal educational qualifications, continuing a formal education process becomes even less enticing. "Watching others succeed in attaining a pastorate with little or no formal education delivers a message to other aspiring pastors that seminary training is not actually necessary in order to respond to the call of God on their lives."[28]

The line of thinking that is the most difficult to fight against is the fact that many black leaders consider traditional white seminaries to harbor long-held racist tendencies in terms of both curriculum and practice. Even in 2015, some leaders believe that

---

26. Ibid., 19.
27. Johnson, "Theological Pathways," 27.
28. Etindi, "Training Ministers," 23.

"negative attitudes—some would call this racism—are still at work in theological schools."[29]

This perceived racism is exhibited through the idea that, in general, black students are unable to complete theological work at the same level as other white students. "Somehow the notion persists that black students can perform only at marginal levels in white theological schools."[30] Unfortunately, some of my personal experiences while pursuing theological higher education could be viewed as validation for this perception.

I was not initially accepted into a doctor of ministry program due to not having a traditional master of divinity degree. I do hold an accredited terminal secular research degree in leadership that required a thesis, as well as an accredited undergraduate degree in Biblical studies and organizational leadership. I also earned an unaccredited doctor of theology degree that required a written dissertation. Additionally, prior to applying to the DMin program, I published a book on leadership that had since been adopted as a textbook in multiple colleges and universities. I also had twenty-one years of ministry experience at the time of my application to the program, including six as lead pastor.

I was admitted to the program only after my pastor, a white man who had a prior relationship with key faculty at the seminary, met face-to-face with the seminary dean and vouched for my skills and ability to conduct research. After being accepted to the program, I discussed this process with black graduates from the institution. Many of them suggested that certain white faculty and staff at the seminary did not believe black students could do the work required to graduate.

One of the reasons black students perceived that this seminary—and others—harbored racist tendencies was because of a lack of racial diversity in the authors and texts used in the curriculum. In fact, "African American ministers have faced the challenge of not getting an education that included their own cultural

---

29. Rooks, "Theological Education and the Black Church," 215.

30. Ibid.

experience."[31] This lack of diversity means that the concerns of black students are likely to be overlooked.

Hinton echoes this concern:

> Also notably absent is the use of texts based on the experience of African-Americans. Given that meaning is ascribed to the phrase "black church," there is an assumption of uniqueness to the worship and expression of faith among black people. Acknowledging the uniqueness of that experience, one would logically expect to find representative texts. To the contrary, while traditional texts may be published to reflect illustrations that resonate with African-Americans, the texts themselves are not different.[32]

This lack of diversity in authors rang true during my experience completing coursework towards my DMin. Only one course within the program utilized a text written by an African American author. There was, however, a diversity of women and Asian authors. This is understandable because the seminary has an active interest in supporting women in ministry. Additionally, the seminary has developed a program of study specifically for students of Korean descent and has also built a partnership with a seminary in Myanmar.

That seminaries should develop curricula and utilize authors that more clearly recognize the needs of black students and more directly address the types of work black students are more likely to engage in is not a new suggestion. In fact, it has been around since at least the 1960s:

> Seminaries need to revise their courses of study in order to prepare students for other than middle-class pastorates. For example, they should devote more attention to the history and tradition of the Negro [sic] churches and should encourage the development of books on this subject. They need to help their Negro students to give more discriminating attention to subjects in the field

---

31. Etindi, "Training Ministers," 33.

32. Hinton, *Commercial Church*, 38.

of Christian social ethics which deal with the socio-economic problems of minority groups.[33]

The fact that this has not been done on a substantial scale is more indication that traditional seminaries are not meeting the unique needs of black students.

It has been suggested that this lack of black representation during the learning process will cause black leaders to do whatever is needed to assimilate to the dominant culture of their seminary experience, which ultimately causes them to become useful to the seminary but useless to the congregations they come from:

> [P]redominately white evangelical denominations and associations have established a cultural context in which the only acceptable blacks, Latinos, and Asians are those who tend to be what some might call "sell-outs," "oreos," "twinkies," and the like—that is, those who are culturally white and tend to separate from their own ethnic communities. The more an ethnic person adopts white cultural norms, leaving his or her ethnic heritage behind. . . the more likely it is that that person will be embraced as a representative of "diversity."[34]

A final spiritual concern many black students hold is that ministry within a black church context requires more than familiarity with a theological doctrine that is widely perceived not to touch people living within the realities of their "now," together with the related idea that formal seminary training instead rewards people for gaining knowledge for knowledge's sake. "Some are frustrated over the tendency of formal education to enrich and perpetuate elitism and meritocracy."[35]

Hinton states this much more extensively when he explains that theology that helps black people is theology that causes life to get better for black people:

33. Rooks, "Vision, Reality and Challenge," 48.

34. Bradley, *Aliens in the Promised Land*, 23.

35. Ward, *Effective Learning*, 76.

It is also important to note that theology in the black church was not the result of reflection and contemplation. Rather, this lived theology fulfilled a very real need among black Americans.

According to Lincoln, "Black theology began with the first sermon preached by a Black slave to his brothers and sisters huddled together in some plantation swamp or forest. It was not a systematic theology which 'hung together in rational patterns of thought,' but it was even then a theology of liberation because it questioned the established contention that God willed the desecration of the human spirit by reducing a man to a thing." The sum of black theology is likely to reflect not only lived experience but also bolsters the human spirit by focusing on the liberation of body and spirit."[36]

In addition to the cultural and spiritual concerns of black students, there are also practical concerns that can deter them from entering traditional theological programs. Students' primary concern is the enormous cost of attending seminary and whether they will be able to secure a position that provides enough income to allow them to pay off their student loans.

The quandary of being able to afford a seminary education is not a new concern. In 1991, more than half of master of divinity graduates had not borrowed for their seminary education, the study found. The average level of debt for borrowers was $11,000, or $14,450 when adjusted for inflation to comparable 2001 figures. Only 1 percent of graduates borrowed more than $30,000. By 2001, only 37 percent of master of divinity graduates had no theological school debt. The average level of debt for borrowers was $25,000, and more than one in five graduates borrowed more than $30,000. . . It is a two-sided problem, denominational officials say, reflecting both the debt acquired to become a minister and the ability to pay it back after graduation. And the two sides increasingly are not adding up.[37]

36. Hinton, *Commercial Church*, 47.

37. Briggs, "Seminary Debt Rising," 1.

Although the challenges related to costs are high for anyone who participates in higher education, they can be even more problematic for black students, who typically make substantially less than their white counterparts. "African American Protestants also have lower income levels than the general public. Almost half of African American Protestants (45%) have household incomes under $30,000, compared to 31% of the total population. Only 17% of black Protestants have household incomes of $75,000 or more, compared to 30% of the general population."[38]

MY PERSONAL EXPERIENCES WITH THEOLOGICAL EDUCATION

I have experienced many of the concerns stated above during my development as a student, minister, and college instructor. I answered my "call" to ministry at the age of sixteen while living in small farming community in Central Texas. I preached my first sermon at age seventeen. My pastor, who was an African American country preacher, had only completed high school. He had answered his call to the ministry less than five years prior to me, and he had been serving as pastor for two years.

There were not many theological resources available within the community we lived within. And I did not realize that there were seminaries and bible colleges and bible institutes where I could become a student. When I was finally introduced to them, the closest Bible Institute was over forty minutes away, and as a high school senior, I was not eligible to enter one anyway.

Access to theological books was also limited. My skills for ministry and personal theology were essentially developed by participating in the life of our church on a weekly basis, by watching my pastor and taking notes so I could imitate him, and by watching televangelists on a weekly basis.

I moved back to St. Louis after graduating high school. Shortly after returning, I began to attend the local accredited community

38. Ibid.

college. After multiple semesters, I found out that an unaccredited Bible institute was located two blocks from my apartment. I simultaneously attended both schools. Eventually, I transferred to an accredited Bible college. While there, I completed a bachelor of science with a double major in Biblical studies and organizational leadership and took a few courses through the affiliated seminary.

During my time at each of these schools, I continued to serve as Associate Minister at multiple black Missionary Baptist churches in the St. Louis metropolitan area. One of my grandfathers was the pastor at one church. As I completed my education, my grandfather, who had only completed high school, felt threatened by my achievements and believed that the congregation might try to oust him and call me as their pastor. This created tension within our relationship, ultimately causing me to leave that church.

I then transferred my membership to a different church whose pastor had become an impromptu mentor for me. This pastor did not have an earned degree, but he could "whoop" and sing. His preaching style from the pulpit was to teach for less than five minutes and to "whoop" for fifteen minutes in order to get an emotional response from congregation members. He often told me that it was unnecessary to go to Bible school because "the Lord would give me what to say as long as I studied the Bible and stayed prayed up."

I eventually left this church and began to serve at churches where my Bible institute and Bible college instructors served as pastors. During this time, I completed a graduate degree at an accredited secular university. After completing that degree, I began to pursue a Doctor of Theology at an unaccredited seminary. I attended this seminary for multiple reasons.

By this time, I was serving as pastor of a small congregation in St. Louis. The congregation agreed with my desire to continue my education, but they could not help pay for it. I could not afford the high tuition of an accredited institution, especially since I was raising a young family and making less than $40,000 per year as a police officer for the City of St. Louis. Additionally, I was still paying off debt from the graduate degree I had earned.

In addition to the financial challenges, I did not feel welcome at any of the other seminaries located in St. Louis because of what I perceived as a lack of respect for black students. This perception was influenced by black students who had attended these seminaries and had less than positive experiences. None of these institutions spoke to the unique heritage that I was raised with as a black person or to the traditions that I experienced within the Missionary Baptist tradition.

I have to admit that I have benefitted from earning all of my degrees, even the unaccredited ones. I have had the opportunity to teach at multiple accredited and unaccredited institutions. Throughout all of these opportunities, I have made a conscious effort to talk to students about their choices in educational institutions and the implications of those choices in their lives.

During these discussions, I use my own personal experiences as a springboard to engage with these topics. I try to consistently discuss differences in curricula and the transferability of credits and degrees obtained at accredited versus unaccredited institutions. I also discuss differences in how black and white congregations view the idea of education and how education can affect opportunities students may or may not have in the future.

Chapter Three

A Brief History of Modes for Providing Theological Training

TRADITIONAL MODELS OF EDUCATION

IDEALLY, I BELIEVE THAT the goal of education is for students to combine a new set of skills and a cache of new information with the skills and information they already possess in order to become better equipped to handle new challenges in the future. As the Reverend Dr. Jawanza Karriem Colvin, EdD, explains, "Individuals learn from their experiences by making connections between knowledge gained from present and previous experiences and using them to consider future implications."[1]

In order for learners to appreciate new skills and information, they must be able to see the benefits of retaining that new knowledge and putting it into practice.

> Learning proceeds best as the learner associates new information with information he already knows. (This is the old and still valid proposition that learning proceeds from the known toward the unknown.) Learning (retention) depends on the use of newly acquired information very soon after it is acquired. Learning also depends on the perceived importance of information.

1. Colvin, "Examination of the Professional Development," 29.

> The importance of information must not only be indicated or demonstrated for the learner, but he must also experience a situation in which he finds that the information relates to his own purposes and goals. Learning (retention and accuracy) is increased when the learner is informed very promptly whether or not his use of new information is appropriate.[2]

There are multiple theories and models that attempt to describe how the learning process occurs. I have identified one theory that seems to be most relevant to the research project at hand. That theory is espoused through a four step-process: "Learning is the process of integrating 'experiences,' 'observations,' 'concepts,' and 'actions' to give direction, provide meaning, and achieve objectives."[3]

The theory progresses in the following cyclical process:

> 1) Concrete Experiences, real-time interaction which engages one's senses and acts as a reference point to test ideas and consider experienced phenomena; 2) Reflective Observation, the process of considering the meaning of experiences based on reasoned deductions and logical inferences and using tools for reflective observation that may include but not be limited to studying, reading, observing, questioning, interviewing, and discourse; 3) Abstract Conceptualization, the development of schemas and concepts which provide a framework for understanding prior and future experiences as well as their possible implications; and 4) Active Experimentation, the testing of schemas and concepts in a concrete experience to verify their usefulness in actual practice.[4]

This framework for learning is especially applicable to this study because it is flexible enough to recognize both formal and nonformal opportunities for learning that occur outside of traditional classroom settings. "Since learning can occur in multiple contextual settings and within varying frameworks, personal and

2. Ward, *Programmed Instruction*, 9.

3. Colvin, "Examination of the Professional Development," 30.

4. Ibid., 30–31.

professional growth can emerge from both the individualized effort of a person to ascertain knowledge as well as from the informal interaction and incidental occurrences which characterize much of human experience."[5]

NONFORMAL MODELS OF LEARNING

In order to understand what nonformal education and learning is, we must understand what it is not. We can do this by contrasting the differences between the formal and nonformal learning processes. According to Dib, formal education "corresponds to a systematic, organized education model, structured and administered according to a given set of laws and norms, presenting a rather rigid curriculum as regards objectives, content and methodology."[6] The hallmark of formal education is structure—structure that determines everything for all parties involved in the learning process.

Dib continues to describe that structure as

> characterized by a contiguous education process named, as Sarramona remarks, "presential education," which necessarily involves the teacher, the students and the institution. It corresponds to the education process normally adopted by our schools and universities. Formal education institutions are administratively, physically and curricularly organized, and require from students a minimum classroom attendance. There is a program that teachers and students alike must observe, involving intermediate and final assessments in order to advance students to the next learning stage. It confers degrees and diplomas pursuant to a quite strict set of regulations.[7]

Nonformal learning is not as structured or restrictive as formal learning. Instead, it is open to the practical needs and desires of the learner. "Non-formal relates more to the motives of

---

5. Ibid., 32.

6. Dib, "Formal, Non-Formal and Informal Education," 1.

7. Ibid.

education than to the modes of education."[8] By recognizing the practical needs of the learner, the material that is learned can eventually be applied by the student. "Formal models of theological education are characterized by the schooling paradigm, whereas nonformal models are not. Rather, nonformal models of theological education are characterized by intentional learning in real-life contexts."[9]

Dib describes nonformal learning in clear contrast to formal learning:

> As seen, formal education has a well-defined set of features. Whenever one or more of these is absent, we may safely state that the educational process has acquired non-formal features. Therefore, if a given education system is not presential most of the time—non-contiguous communication—we may say that it has non-formal education features. Likewise, non-formal education characteristics are found when the adopted strategy does not require student attendance, decreasing the contacts between teacher and student and most activities take place outside the institution—as for instance, home reading and paperwork. Educative processes endowed with flexible curricula and methodology, capable of adapting to the needs and interests of students, for which time is not a pre-established factor but is contingent upon the student's work pace, certainly do not correspond to those comprised by formal education, but fit into the so-called non-formal education.[10]

Nonformal education contains a level of flexibility that benefits learners and recognizes that the individual goals of a learner may not necessarily be driven by the expectation of earning a specific degree, but may be motivated instead by a simple desire to improve themselves and their community.

---

8. Ward, *Effective Learning*, 72.

9. Kemp, "Church-Based Theological Education," 1.

10. Dib, "Formal, Non-Formal and Informal Education," 2.

[T]ypically in a non-formal environment—intermediate rewards are not utilized or are much less important than they are in formal education. Symbolic rewards, certificates, degrees and so forth (the pay-offs that you can't eat but that you are taught to hold in high regard in formal education), are virtually inconsequential . . . Non-formal education tends to be oriented to a reward system that is closer to the world of work and to the improvement of the quality of everyday life.[11]

Regardless of whether the learning process is formal or non-formal, those leading the education process must make sure that learning is relevant to the needs of the student.

Effective learning depends on: (1) relevancy of the educational goals to social values, (2) accommodation of the learning characteristics of learners, and (3) accommodation of the pedagogical expectations of the learners. Thus those who are concerned about effective learning (whether the educational setting is formal or non-formal) must evaluate the relevancy of the educational experiences to social values. They must also be careful to select materials, procedures and methods that are appropriate to the characteristics, goals and expectations of the learners.[12]

GOAL OF NONFORMAL EDUCATION

The primary goal of nonformal education is to meet the practical learning needs of students: "Non-formal education is typically concerned with learning that has a high degree of 'practical' usefulness. Thus the specifications of learning. . . would be especially concerned with the learning in exactly the form it will be most likely applied. . . The learning would be specified in terms of its practical use, not in terms of abstract or theoretical understandings."[13]

11. Ward, *Effective Learning*, 4–5.

12. Ibid., 74.

13. Ibid., 80.

This goal recognizes that formal educational processes can actually be a hindrance to potential learners for multiple reasons. Nonformal educational options may be more effective because they have more flexibility "to bring education to people who are not being reached by the formal educational establishment, to provide education at lower cost, or to direct educational efforts toward goals that are more practical or more closely related to the learner's needs within their society."[14]

BENEFITS OF NONFORMAL EDUCATION

The benefits of nonformal education are numerous. I will highlight a few of them. First, nonformal education provides learners with the opportunity to more intently focus on personal goals and desired outcomes from the learning process. "From this position, non-formal education is far more than new delivery systems; it is the restructuring of goals and even the underlying assumptions about what constitutes worthwhile content in education."[15]

Second, nonformal learning opportunities allow the student and his or her goals be the focus instead of the teacher or a curriculum that may need serious evaluation.

> Occasionally we need to be reminded that schools do not make people learn. Schools may help people learn; certainly schools can provide opportunities to learn; and schools can even help people become more interested in learning. But schools in general are but the way to bring people into contact with educational resources. Whether or not the people learn and what may be the value of what they learn are issues sometimes overlooked. . . Assuring effective learning demands that ends and means (goals and procedures) must be aligned.[16]

Third, nonformal learning recognizes the learner's desire for a practical education and provides that education through an

14. Ibid., 77.
15. Ibid.
16. Ibid., 73–74.

atmosphere that encourages personal initiative. As Ward explains, "Whether the learning takes place through informal tutoring, supervised on the job training, apprenticeship or by listening to stories and legends recounted by elders, the informally learned individual is primarily discovery-oriented and is usually operating at a concrete level of mental operations." That is, "the informal learner is exposed to and searches out answers to concrete problems."[17]

WHAT THIS MEANS TO THOSE WHO SEEK TO EDUCATE AFRICAN AMERICAN BAPTIST PASTORS AND LEADERS

Based on the divergent lived histories of black and white communities, each group views theological and leadership education differently. In a white context, a person's ability to serve in a ministry position may be based on the degrees they hold. The opposite is true within a black context: "A non-schooled adult is not always unlearned or uneducated."[18] This allows a certain level of opportunity in the black church that may not be present in white churches.

In white circles, entrance into ministry can be based on personal choice and a desire to serve in a particular ministry position. Within the black church, entrance into the ministry is predicated on a "call" from God. Within a white context, obtaining a level of education that allows a person to understand and communicate theological terms may be the primary indicator of that person's ability to serve in ministry.

Within a black context, a person's ability to preach in such a way that recognizes the past experiences of black people while reminding them that God is ever present and preparing to do something on their behalf in the future is the primary measurement of success. The ability to preach this message is not necessarily learned in a formal classroom setting.

17. Ibid., 27.
18. Ibid., 26.

Because of the clear variance in experience and focus between black and white churches, it may not be realistic to think that black pastors and leaders have to obtain training from traditional white seminaries in order to faithfully lead their congregations:

> It is unlikely that religious education in the black church will be the same as religious education in white churches. Nor should that be the goal. The unique experience of African Americans in the U.S., and the unique role of the church in the lives of African Americans may demand different content and processes. Religious education will and should be driven by the unique experience of blacks in the United States.[19]

With this in mind, a valid option for traditional theological institutions may be to examine the long-held processes found within the black church tradition in order to see if some of those processes can be replicated and incorporated into institutionalized learning.

> Within every society there are sources in the traditions and the value systems that have given rise to what education has become. That which a culture has produced cannot be overlooked in the planning of something new. Whether education is a matter of elaborate institutionalized efforts or merely the simplicity of familial and tribal influences, rituals and indoctrinations, the sources are in the history and in the cultural milieu of the society. Before attempting to augment or significantly alter the educational resources of a community, region, or nation, these sources must be examined and, to the extent possible, understood.[20]

Additionally, traditional institutions can seek the input of African American leaders and learners in order to develop learning initiatives and processes that more adequately address students' needs and desires, instead of the institution telling students they have to learn a specific set of information—even if that

19. Hinton, *Commercial Church*, 220.
20. Ward, *Effective Learning*, 119.

information and the learning process itself hold no relevance to the contexts those learners and leaders serve.

> Of all the many variables in an instructional system, the target population is likely to be the most complex. The three sets of factors that must be understood are (1) the motivations that drive the learners and the sorts of psycho-socio-economic rewards that will sustain them as learners; (2) the habits and expectations that their previous learning experiences have induced; and (3) the styles of mental processes and learning characteristics that have been induced by previous formal and informal learning experiences.[21]

Recognizing and understanding these three core principles is key to providing educational opportunities that will best benefit African American pastors and leaders.

21. Ibid.

Chapter Four

Why Should Leadership Development Be Important to Black Leaders?

THEOLOGICAL, BIBLICAL, AND HISTORICAL GROUNDING

The Work of the Spirit Accomplished through Leaders

ONE OF THE REGULAR tasks leaders of congregations face is to help congregants understand the truths that are conveyed through God's Word and how to regularly experience communion with the Holy Spirit in order to convey God's love in this world. Understanding these truths and participating in communion with the Spirit can lead to spiritual growth for a congregation. Understanding and communion can also lead to a congregation that better understands itself and its calling to both a specific physical community and to one another.

> How do we help clergy and other congregational leaders learn to talk across the cultural divides that exist within our congregations? With intermarriage, denominational switching, higher education, career mobility and the complex spiritual pilgrimages taken by so many church members, one cannot assume that members and leaders

share a worldview. In addition to learning to identify who and what is in the room with us, we need to learn to work with cultural diversity, to negotiate differences, to bring to the surface hidden values, and to turn congregations into places of healthy cultural exchange.[1]

One of the means that the Holy Spirit uses to bring all of creation into relationship with God is the work of local congregations. One way for congregations to be aware of this—and be ready to actively cooperate with the work of the Spirit—is for congregants to be trained to recognize and understand the movement of the Spirit by their leaders. In order for leaders to be able to recognize the Spirit's movement themselves and be able to train their congregants as well, leaders need access to training that is informed by their particular contexts.

By participating in an intentional process that seeks to develop their overall ministry and leadership skills, participants can be introduced to information that challenges long-held assumptions about what it means to be in ministry even as they become informed of best practices identified as worthy of consideration across multiple contexts.

The Work of the Spirit Accomplished through Time

God's Spirit was present throughout the creation process, and it is still present and active in the world today. In the beginning, the Spirit, sent forth by God, facilitated the process of creation. As the breath of God, the Spirit carried God's creative and life-generating powers into what was to be. The Spirit, sent forth by the Source, created what had previously not been as it hovered over the earth, formed its intimate parts, and established a home for God and people to experience lively interdependence together.

The Spirit then participated in the creation of humans. After being breathed out by God, the Spirit flowed into and through Adam and Eve at their conception and filled them with life. These

1. Carroll, "How Do Pastors Practice Leadership?," 1.

previously empty vessels would eventually procreate and populate the earth. What had been breathed into them was then passed on to their children and to future generations. Because the Spirit was so intimately involved in the creation process and passed a portion of its essence to created beings, the Spirit made it possible for all of creation to be filled with a portion of God's presence and to taste the divine.

The Spirit's filling of Adam and Eve lent a portion of God's Spirit to the created being. This share was not earned or merited, but it was given instead as a good-faith effort on God's behalf towards humankind. The Spirit's action was a gift given within relationship. It ensured relatedness between the human spirit and the Spirit. This relatedness was not a possession or birthright of humankind, but rather a confirmation from God concerning relationship between the holy and the human.

Furthermore, the Spirit's filling was an influencing factor that ensures future generations will have a natural alignment towards the holy. God's decision to share God's breath meant that future generations would be born with the desire and the opportunity to share in the relationship God wants. Additionally, humans are able to share a connectedness with one another, since all of our human spirits have a trace of the divine. This shared inner desire can lead us all to strike out on a common journey. That journey is a search for completeness. This search for completeness can be fulfilled only in connectedness with God.

Along with the other members of the Trinity, God's Spirit currently works to restore all of creation's relationships with God. By the power of the Spirit, humanity and all creation are moving towards a renewed relationship of peaceful cohabitation. The Spirit's actions in this world take into account the needs of the world, which has suffered unduly for actions it did not commit.

In Rev 21, John, under the guidance of the Spirit, prophesied the healing and restorative transformation that would occur for all of creation. A new heaven and a new earth would become concrete experiences for all to see. God would be present with humankind, causing pain and fear to be removed from human existence. The almighty Creator would not allow his handiwork to remain stained and broken.

Not only will physical creation be redeemed, but humans will experience redemption as well. God, through Christ, provided atonement for people, including forgiveness and restoration to the family of God. Although renewed relationship with God is available, the Spirit is still changing humankind, just as the world is being changed, into what we shall one day fully be. As with the rest of creation, we shall one day be more than we are today. One day, we will more fully bear the image of God in our actions and being. This process began through God establishing and maintaining a relationship with a peculiar people as testified in Deut 26:18: "Since you have agreed to obey the LORD, he has agreed that you will be his people and that you will belong to him, just as he promised."

The Spirit participated in the lives of the ancient Hebrew people, moving in what we may consider to be limited, although intentional, ways by overshadowing specific people for specific durations of time to accomplish specific goals that would lead to special events within history. Examples of this overshadowing include but are not limited to Noah building the ark, Moses leading God's people out of Egypt, Samson slaying the enemies of God's people, and other Old Testament judges who, like Shamgar, were instrumental in protecting God's children. The Spirit used the individual actions of singular people for corporate good. The ultimate corporate good would be that these people would be gathered to God and formed into God's own people.

Later, in the lives of God's followers who eagerly anticipated the coming of Messiah, the Spirit caused men and women to proclaim and confirm the presence of the prophesied Messiah that was to be born through Mary. In the life of the early church, the Comforter, previously alluded to by Christ, caused the still-forming body of Christ to exhibit ecstatic gifts as signs of believers' relationship with God and the fulfillment of Christ's promises to make them into Christ's body. As with prior generations, one of the Spirit's goals was to form people into a community that would be God's own and participate in worship sustained by community members' reconciled relationship with their Creator.

Today, the Spirit continues to serve as the mediator between people as we grow in our connection to God and to one another. First Corinthians says, "But God has given us his Spirit. That's why we don't think the same way that the people of this world think. That's also why we can recognize the blessings that God has given us" (1 Cor 2:12). The Spirit serves as our encourager as we grow in becoming the body of Christ and come to look more like him in both action and attitude. By the Spirit, we are able to be joined to God in relationships of love and partnership, which ultimately leads us to reflect God's presence in our relationship with God's creation. The Spirit serves as the facilitating agent in these processes of being conformed to the image of God.

This connection to God and one another is made available to all. Although in prior times God, through the Spirit, chose to use specific people for specific purposes, the Spirit has not discriminated against anyone in the process of bridging the gap between God and people. The foundation for this connection to God is God's love for creation and God's desire for relationship with that creation. One way for people to learn this truth is through the work of the Holy Spirit within the context of local congregations. It is the task of the corporate church and individual congregations to share this good news.

The Work of the Spirit Accomplished through the Church

Scripture teaches that the church is to be light in the world and that it is tasked with sharing its message of God's love. It is tasked with bearing the likeness, or reflection, of its Savior. The church is one of God's ways of expressing God's desire to see fully restored relationships between the holy and human. The church exists to show the world how God communicates God's self through Jesus Christ, as well as how humankind should respond to God's work of salvation and the coming of the kingdom of God.

In simple terms, the kingdom of God refers to a time that is both present and future, a time when the world and all that is in it will be changed for the glory of God. It's presently occurring, and it will occur in the future, in the sense that God is working through people to change and transform that which was fallen and turned into something not intended. Paul Borden, a pastor and denominational leader, notes, "The Church of Jesus Christ was designed by its founder to bring about the kingdom of God, which means to effectively challenge the work, intention, and kingdom of the evil one. Therefore, the very nature and essence of the Church is to be involved in the effort of turning lost people into fully devoted followers of Jesus Christ."[2]

Within the kingdom of God, God sees and treats everyone equally. Life empowered by the Spirit makes it possible for us to see one another in new ways that reveal our equality as well. We are able to recognize that God's kingdom is being revealed through diverse cultures and societies, religions, and histories as they reflect love, compassion, and healing. We are also able to recognize that God does not require uniformity in the coming kingdom.

As it will be in the kingdom, so it is already in the Spirit. Social standing becomes irrelevant. Within the Spirit, there is no rank or order based on superiority or inferiority. As it will be in the kingdom, so it already is in the Spirit. No one is dominant or subordinate. No one is on the inside while others sit outside. The field is leveled for all to have equal footing.

Leaders are called to teach their congregations that everyone is

> . . . created by God to be God's primary tool for making individual disciples and for changing entire communities. God expects local churches to take on the stewardship of changing the social and political structures of their communities, primarily through the evangelism of individuals and then by helping these individuals live out their new lives together in Christ as they work to bring near the kingdom of God. If this is so, then the pastor's

2. Borden, *Direct Hit*, 347–52.

primary leadership responsibility under God is directed more to the congregation as an entity than it is to the individuals who comprise the congregation. Such a stewardship only happens as pastors act as transformational leaders, developing and surrounding themselves with other transformational leaders.[3]

The Work of the Spirit Accomplished through Theological Education

My hope is that participation in a theological education program will result in leaders who are educated in a way that insures their particular contexts are not ignored but are instead embraced, respected, and incorporated into the learning process. This change should in turn increase leaders' ability to move their particular congregations into a stronger relationship with God through the leading of the Holy Spirit and to become more missional in both thought and action.

3. Ibid., 180–84.

Chapter Five

How Did I Come up with the Data?

RESEARCH DESIGN AND PROCEDURES

THE RESEARCH PROCESS WAS initiated to answer the question "Based on the unique needs of African American Baptist pastors and leaders studied, what is the most effective process to provide them with ministry and leadership development training in order for them to become more effective in performing their duties within their ministry contexts?"

This project involved identifying and understanding practices currently used within African American Baptist churches and their related educational entities. It also involved identifying and understanding what practitioners understand to be the best ways to learn ministry skills, as well as ascertaining the level of satisfaction and motivation experienced by those pastors and leaders who attempt to implement the new skills they learn.

In order to adequately address the overall research question, I needed to develop a way to learn the training processes of the African American Baptist pastors and leaders. I chose to do this within my own context: the St. Louis metropolitan area.

WHAT IS ST. LOUIS LIKE?

Like many other major metropolitan areas, the City of St. Louis and the larger St. Louis metropolitan region are divided by implicit and explicit racial and economic lines. St. Louis's history is filled with instances of racial discrimination and racial unrest. One of the most polarizing legal cases that began in St. Louis was the Dred Scott case in which a slave sued for his freedom after his master died. Ultimately, the United States Supreme Court ruled against Scott, stating that under the US Constitution, blacks had no rights that white people needed to respect.

Another famous instance of racial unrest is found in the East St. Louis riots that occurred in May and July of 1917. East St. Louis is located across the Mississippi River from St. Louis and is considered to be a part of the metropolitan area. During the months of May and July of 1917, an estimated 3,000 white men attacked and killed between 100–200 black people and destroyed entire neighborhoods within the black community over frustrations with African American migration to the area and black participation in the local labor force. In response to this aggression, blacks retaliated by killing two men who were eventually found to be police officers. These two killings led to more attacks by organized white labor and the destruction of more black neighborhoods.

Most recently, the area has undergone more racial unrest following the shooting of an unarmed black youth named Michael Brown by a white police officer named Darren Wilson. This shooting led to racially motivated rioting, protests, and overall discord. The subsequent investigations launched after the incident revealed a region-wide disparity in how minorities are treated by law enforcement compared to how whites are treated by law enforcement.

The St. Louis region is not only divided along racial lines, it is also divided along economic lines. Within the region, minorities are two times likelier to be poor compared to whites. Minorities are less likely to graduate high school than whites. Minorities are also less likely to have access to needed resources that help to improve their quality of life than whites.[1]

Much of this disparity is caused by "white flight," the practice of white families leaving racially and economically integrated areas for locations that have less racial and economic diversity. When this occurs, much-needed resources and consistent tax revenue streams typically leave those areas as well, leaving those who remain in challenging social and economic conditions. Over the last sixty years, St. Louis has lost more than 500,000 residents.[2]

With this economic, racial, and social history in mind, it is not surprising that even religious life in St. Louis is still, for the most part, segregated. Although my intent is not to deal with the overall issue of lingering racial segregation in St. Louis or in St. Louis churches, the reality of such segregation's continued existence means that it does affect how black leaders view educational opportunities that originate from a historically white educational institution. This, in turn, provides an opportunity for a new educational process to occur that better meets the needs of black pastors and leaders.

Because of the racial tension that still exists in the region, many black leaders still do not believe that white educational professionals value or respect the experiences of blacks and subsequently do not believe that these types of institutions can adequately prepare black leaders for the unique challenges that exist within the black church and black community.

Within the St. Louis metropolitan area, there are at least 528 churches that identify as African American or black.[3] Within those 528 identified churches, 154 have identified themselves as African American Baptist.[4]

Based on this sizable number of churches, I concluded that I would not be able to adequately capture the full extent of professional development experiences of all the pastors and leaders

1. City of St. Louis, "Brief History of the City of St. Louis."
2. Ibid.
3. Eugene, *Black Church St. Louis*, 1.
4. Ibid.

associated with these churches. However, I determined that an in-depth probe into the educational experiences of a smaller segment of this population would provide a perspective for understanding the experiences of the members of the overall group.

This process occurred through four phases that sought input from individual pastors and leaders who were seeking educational opportunities, as well as from pastors and leaders who were responsible for providing educational opportunities to learners.

PHASE 1: PILOT SURVEY AND FOCUS GROUPS

Research into this smaller segment of the identified population was conducted over a two-year span through two distinct processes that incorporated two separate groups of participants. The first process began via traditional mail and through email correspondence. Through these modes, I issued a general request to pastors and leaders I knew to be interested in educational opportunities that would help them improve their ministry skills. The participants were asked to complete a pilot survey that sought to understand the educational experiences of Baptist pastors and leaders located in the St. Louis area.

The intent of the survey was to identify general criteria about Baptist pastors and leaders such as ministry position held, number of years serving in ministry, gender, race, highest level of education completed, how often they performed duties related to their ministry position, how they learned to perform those duties, highest level of education completed by their pastor or mentor, and whether they regularly participated in some type of continuing education program. The pilot survey was completed by 29 participants.

In addition to the pilot survey, I also conducted two separate focus groups. The two groups differed in multiple ways. The first group was made up of eight pastors who had served in their positions for over ten years. The second group was made up of seven ministers and leaders who had less than ten years of experience in their positions. Participants were invited to participate by email and face-to-face invitation. Thirty people were invited to participate. Fifteen people participated.

The intent of the focus groups was to gain in-depth information about specific practices related to training pastors and leaders for the ministry and discover how those being trained responded to the techniques used to train them. The questions asked during each focus group were aimed at understanding what participants thought were the most important areas of ministry to be trained in, the best ways to train pastors and leaders to perform these duties, how participants trained or planned to train future pastors and leaders, and how participants themselves were trained to perform their ministry duties.

The first focus group contained eight members. The second focus group contained seven members. These focus groups occurred during the summer of 2012. The data collected from these two focus groups was accumulated and analyzed during the fall of 2012.

PHASE 2: QUESTIONNAIRES AND INTERVIEWS

The second process for researching a smaller segment of the population of pastors and leaders in the St. Louis area was conducted in the fall of 2014 through one questionnaire issued to members of two distinct Baptist districts and members of the Missionary Baptist Ministers Union of St. Louis and Vicinity, as well as through interviews with the moderators of those two distinct Baptist Unions and the president of the Missionary Baptist Convention of the State of Missouri.

These particular groups were chosen based on the diversity of members' experience as pastors and leaders as well as the diversity of members' educational experiences. Participants held membership within the two prominent Baptist districts that serve the region: the Missionary Baptist Ministers Union of St. Louis and Vicinity and the Missionary Baptist State Convention, which serves Missionary Baptist churches within the entire state of Missouri. Only two people that participated in the surveys and focus groups of Phase 1 contributed to the questionnaires and interviews of Phase 2.

A Baptist district is a group of Baptist churches that voluntarily agree to associate with each other based on common beliefs in faith, practice, and polity. Within the St. Louis area, there are at least seven distinct Baptist districts. These Baptist districts can serve as a local source of accountability, camaraderie, education, and encouragement for pastors and leaders. The district with the largest number of member churches in the region is the Antioch Baptist District.

Additionally, I have a personal relationship with the moderators (presidents) of these two districts. Based on these factors, I chose them as participants in the research project. I was allowed to present a questionnaire to pastors and leaders within the Antioch Baptist District and to members of the Union Baptist District. Data collected from these two districts were accumulated and analyzed.

The Missionary Baptist Ministers Union of St. Louis and Vicinity is a group of pastors and ministers that voluntarily meet once a week to participate in fellowship, mutual encouragement, and educational lectures. The Ministers Union claims over 100 pastors and ministers as members. Weekly attendance at meetings is approximately forty members. I am a member of the Ministers Union and was allowed to distribute questionnaires to Ministers Union members. Data collected from this group was accumulated and analyzed. The questionnaire distributed to members of the Ministers Union was the same questionnaire distributed to members of the Antioch and Union Baptist Districts.

The questions proposed to the participants of these groups sought to understand ministry position held, years of service in that position, participants' opinion of the five most important areas of service to the local church, how often they participated in those areas of service, how participants learned to perform those functions, the highest level of education participants' completed, whether participants had been able to apply what they learned through their educational programs, whether participants had a mentor, whether that mentoring relationship provided them with skills to perform certain ministry tasks, and whether they were involved in continuing education.

In addition to questionnaires issued to members of the Baptist districts, the moderators of both districts were interviewed to gain specific insight into how each district viewed theological education and the process each district had adopted related to it. I initiated these two interviews with much anticipation because, in addition to enjoying a personal relationship with both of the moderators, I appreciated the value of their vastly different personal experiences related to participation in traditional theological education.

Although one moderator had participated in various forms of traditional theological education, he had not completed an accredited degree program or a traditional theological educational program. On the opposite end of the spectrum, the other moderator had earned an accredited master of divinity, doctor of ministry, and juris doctorate. The interview questions presented were created after obtaining results from the initial surveys that were distributed and collected. The interview questions sought to gain more detailed information than was acquired through the surveys.

The final portion of this second process involved interviewing the president of the Missionary Baptist State Convention of Missouri. The president is the most powerful Missionary Baptist in the state of Missouri because he holds great influence over the majority of Missionary Baptist pastors and leaders in the state. The president is elected to this position by his peers for a term of three years. His views and opinions set the tone for the majority of Missionary Baptists in the state. Ultimately, his opinion and actions in relation to theological education set the tone for churches located in the St. Louis region.

Interview questions proposed to the president sought to understand the views and practices of the State Convention as it relates to the importance of education, how ministers and leaders are taught to perform ministry functions, the form training programs take, the frequency of training programs, the educational requirements for those who train other pastors and leaders, and how these training programs are evaluated by students.

PHASE 3: FINALIZATION

The final phase of the project accomplished the task of combining the accumulated data in order to analyze it and to identify patterns and themes related to the needs and desires of pastors and leaders in their particular contexts. Additionally, the data revealed the educational opportunities currently available to Missionary Baptist pastors and leaders, as well as respondents' level of participation and satisfaction with those opportunities.

Chapter Six

What Did the Data Show?

PHASE 1A: PILOT SURVEY

THE INTENT OF THE pilot survey was to identify general criteria about Baptist pastors and leaders such as ministry position held, number of years served in ministry, gender, race, highest level of education completed, frequency with which they performed duties related to their ministry position, how they learned to perform those duties, highest level of education completed by their pastor or mentor, and whether they regularly participated in some type of continuing education program. The pilot survey was completed by twenty-nine participants who all had various levels of experience participating in traditional and nontraditional theological education.

The following tables summarize results from the pilot survey.

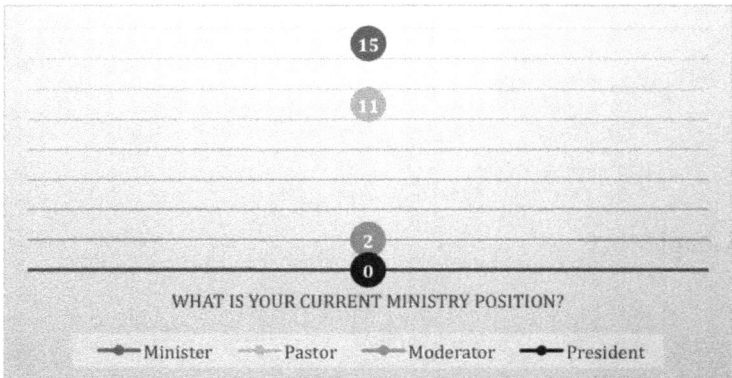

Table 1. Results of Pilot Survey Question 1

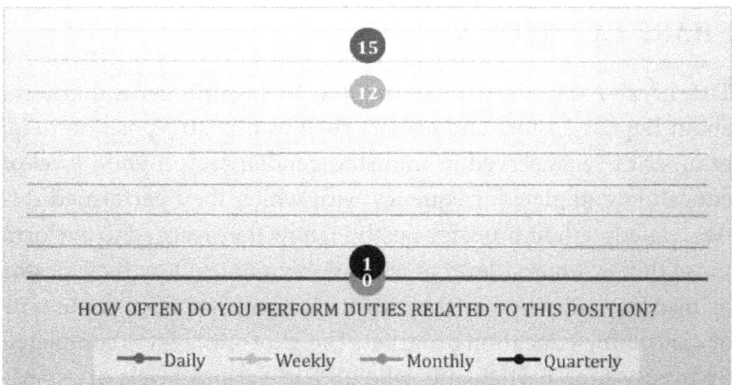

Table 2. Results of Pilot Survey Question 3

As Table 1 shows, a little over half of the respondents identified themselves as ministers, meaning that they served in some ministry capacity other than pastor. The remaining respondents identified themselves as pastors. Moderators are pastors who lead a district of churches that voluntarily fellowship together. Table 2 shows that more than half of the respondents performed duties related to their ministry position on a daily basis.

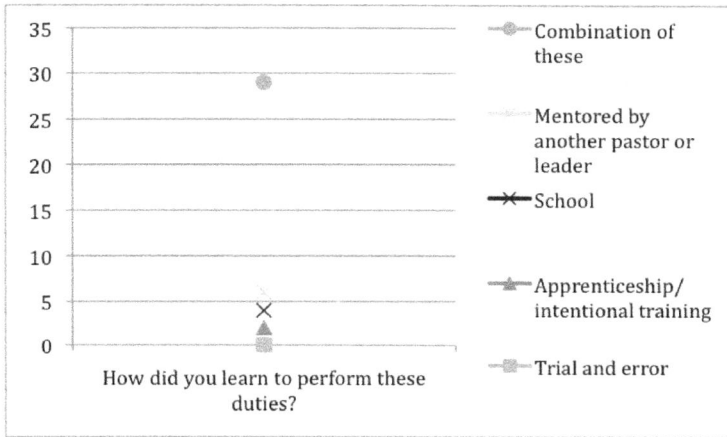

Table 3. Results of Pilot Survey Question 4

As seen in Table 3, respondents stated overwhelmingly that they learned how to perform their duties in ministry through multiple processes, including being mentored by a more knowledgeable pastor or leader, participation in a standardized educational program, and being allowed to learn from mistakes they made while fulfilling their duties. This means that the respondents have learned the value of participating in multiple modes of ministry development.

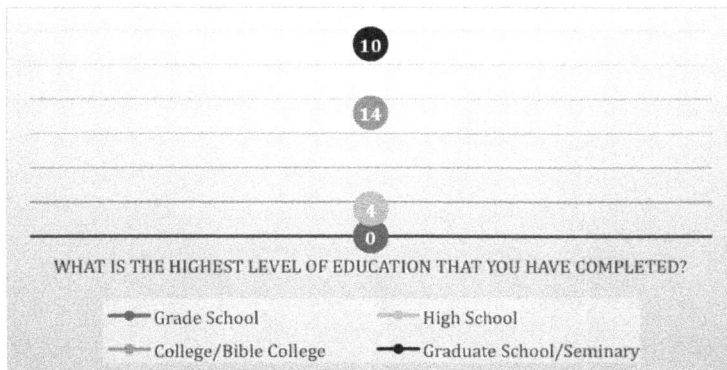

Table 4. Results of Pilot Survey Question 6

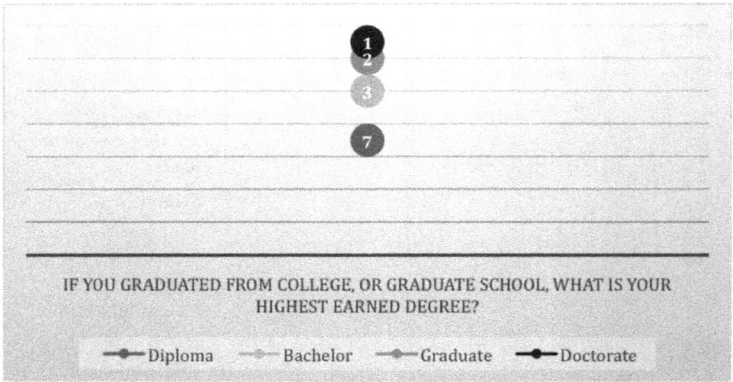

IF YOU GRADUATED FROM COLLEGE, OR GRADUATE SCHOOL, WHAT IS YOUR HIGHEST EARNED DEGREE?

Diploma   Bachelor   Graduate   Doctorate

Table 5. Results of Pilot Survey Question 7

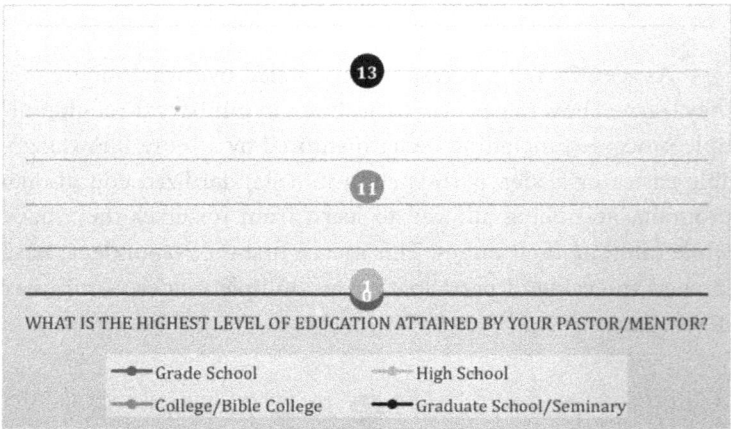

WHAT IS THE HIGHEST LEVEL OF EDUCATION ATTAINED BY YOUR PASTOR/MENTOR?

Grade School   High School
College/Bible College   Graduate School/Seminary

Table 6. Results of Pilot Survey Question 9

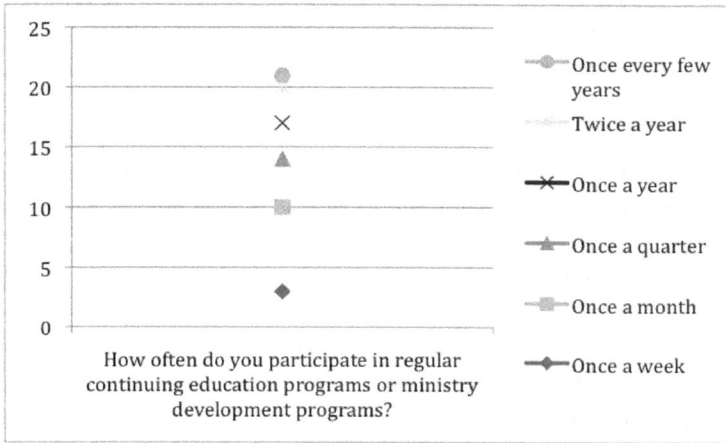

Table 7. Results of Pilot Survey Question 10

According to the data shown in Tables 4, 5, 6, and 7, an overwhelming majority of respondents, as well as their mentors, have participated in some type of college program and, at a minimum, successfully completed those program requirements in order to earn a diploma. Additionally, respondents participated in some type of continuing education program once every three months. This means that the majority of respondents and their mentors recognize the value of participating in a standardized educational program and have successfully completed the requirements of those programs.

PHASE 1B: FOCUS GROUPS

In addition to the pilot survey, I facilitated two separate focus groups. The intent of the focus groups was to gain in-depth information about specific practices related to training pastors and leaders for the ministry and how those being trained responded to the techniques used to train them. The questions asked during the focus groups sought to understand what participants thought were the most important areas of ministry to be trained in, the best ways to train pastors and leaders to perform these duties, how participants trained or planned to train future pastors and leaders, and how participants themselves were trained to perform their ministry duties.

I submitted requests to forty pastors and leaders to participate in a focus group. The only respondents to this request were eight members of a pastors fellowship who met voluntarily on a weekly basis to encourage each other through fellowship, mutual encouragement, and interaction with the Bible through directed Bible study and preaching.

At the time these focus groups were conducted, this fellowship was made up of fourteen senior pastors and one associate pastor. Each participant had at least ten years of experience as a pastor. I was a member of this pastors group. The second focus group was made up of seven students who were participating in a ministry formation certificate program through an accredited seminary. Each member of the second focus group had less than ten years of experience in ministry.

The following four questions were posed to the focus groups in an attempt to find out what they thought were the most effective ways to train future leaders. The questions presented were as follows:

1. What are the three most important areas in which people need to be trained for effective ministry?

2. What are the three best ways to train future ministers/ pastors/preachers?

3. What do you do/would you do to train future ministers/pastors/preachers in your church?

4. How were you trained?

In general, the focus groups revealed shared expectations and hopes each group had concerning the training process that occurs in Missionary Baptist churches in St. Louis. Individual members of each group independently stated that a clear understanding of the Bible and its related doctrines was the most important qualification for a leader within the church to have. Effective skills in communicating what the Bible says (the skills of teaching and preaching) were considered to be the next most important ability for any leader to exhibit. Being trained to have a regular and active personal prayer life was identified as the third most important qualification.

Other areas of importance identified were

- how to conduct pastoral care (showing ethical care for congregation members);
- how to be accountable to other people;
- how to disciple lost and/or new believers;
- how to get along with other people within the church; and
- how to be better organized in order to handle the responsibilities of leadership roles.

The two groups also agreed on what they thought were the three best ways to train future ministry leaders. According to participants, the best approach is to give future ministry leaders regular opportunities to participate in the daily and weekly life of their congregation. Giving future ministry leaders regular opportunities to participate in a leadership role will enable them to gain confidence in both themselves and from the people to whom they minister. Additionally, these future leaders will be able to learn from and fix mistakes and/or try new techniques while leading.

The second best approach identified by the group to train leaders was to allow them to participate in an intentional internship process. This internship process can take multiple forms, one being a regular leadership class led by a seasoned pastor or other qualified pastoral staff member. Within such a program, the group revealed that specific goals should be set, as well as clearly defined parameters of operation/responsibility for novice leaders. An added benefit of this type of program is that it would relieve the mentor and the mentee of certain pressures and expectations by setting clear boundaries.

The third best approach the participants surfaced was participation in some type of academic program—whether it is a program within a Bible college, seminary, or through an entity associated with a local congregation, such as monthly learning opportunities through a local Baptist district or yearly programs through the National Congress of Christian Education, the educational arm of national Baptist entities. The general consensus was that it would be beneficial to participate in some type of directed study program that has as its goal moving participants from one level of academic knowledge to a higher level.

Two surprises came out of the focus groups. The most notable surprise was that most of the students participating in the ministry formation certificate program did not have an intentional training program in place at their home church. Because of this, most of the learners saw the certificate program as one of the most beneficial sources of their ministry development.

The second surprise coincided with this first finding. Most of the pastors who participated in the focus group through the pastors fellowship did not have an intentional process for training leaders within their congregations. They all gave leaders within their congregations multiple opportunities to serve, but when it came to teaching specific information or sharing tools and techniques related to leadership, the majority of these pastors sent their staff somewhere else to receive training. The reason for this decision was that most of those pastors did not feel adequately prepared to manage leadership training because they had not graduated from a college themselves.

What the Data from Phase 1 Shows

From the data collected through Phase 1, I learned that pastors and leaders attribute high value to participating in a mentoring relationship with a person who has more relevant experience than they do. They also place value on participating in some type of standardized educational program that either occurs within their home congregation or through another Baptist entity that has an ongoing working relationship with their home congregation. Finally, they place value on participating in some type of ongoing professional development through their home church or an entity affiliated with their church.

PHASE 2A: MINISTRY QUESTIONNAIRE

Phase 2A consisted of distributing questionnaires, in person, to members of two distinct Missionary Baptist Districts and members of one Pastors and Ministers Union in St. Louis. These groups are made up of pastors and leaders who have varying levels of experiences related to theological education. This Pastors and Ministers Union is a stand-alone organization that is completely different from the pastors fellowship identified in Phase 1. 60 questionnaires were distributed by hand at three different meetings. Twenty three were completed and submitted.

The questions proposed to these participants sought to build upon the findings from prior instruments implemented and to gain further information related to ministry position held, years of service in that position, the participant's opinion of the five most important areas of service to the local church, how often he/she participated in those areas of service, how participants learned to perform those functions, highest level of education completed, whether participants have been able to apply what was learned through educational programs, whether participants had a mentor, whether that mentoring relationship provided them with skills to perform certain ministry tasks, and whether they were involved in continuing education.

The following tables summarize the results of the questionnaire.

Number of Years of Experience

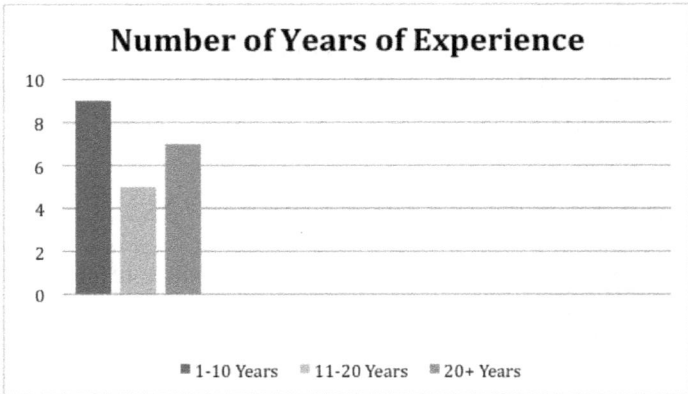

■ 1-10 Years ■ 11-20 Years ■ 20+ Years

Table 8: Results of Baptist Leadership Questionnaire for Question 2

From the research sample, I learned that 56 percent of respondents were senior or lead pastors. Additionally, according to the data results shown in Table 8, there was great diversity in the number of years respondents had served in ministry. Forty-two percent had served less than ten years, 33 percent had served for more than twenty years, and 23 percent had served between eleven and nineteen years.

Based on data acquired during Phase 1, I determined that preaching, teaching, pastoral care for church members, leadership/management of church business, and administration were the five most important skills needed for Missionary Baptist pastors and leaders in St. Louis. Participants were provided with definitions for terms on the questionnaire, and participants were allowed to ask questions to clarify any information in the questionnaire. When participants were asked to rank these skills in order of most important to least important, Phase 2 respondents ranked them from most to least important as follows:

5. *Preaching:* Occurs as part of a traditional formal worship service (Sunday morning or evening, Wednesday evening, or funerals) and consists of the speaker communicating from the Bible to listeners in order for them to hear what God thinks about a certain subject. There may be interaction between

speaker and listener during the preaching process. Also, the one preaching must be called of God to perform this task.

6. *Teaching:* Teaching is less formal than preaching and occurs as part of an intentional process of spiritual development any given day of the week. There is regular and informal interaction between the teacher and the one being taught. Anyone who has obtained a certain level of education or practical spiritual maturity can teach.

7. *Pastoral Care for Members:* The process of meeting the practical daily needs of congregation members through visitation, phone calls, and written communications.

8. *Leadership/Management of Church Business:* The ability to effectively work within the business and/or financial side of an organization or congregation in order to make sure that regular legal and financial responsibilities are met.

9. *Administration:* The ability to direct and manage congregational staff and volunteers as they fulfill their respective duties.

According to respondents, preaching, teaching, leadership/management, and administration duties are performed primarily on a weekly basis, while pastoral care is performed on a daily basis.

As with respondents who completed the initial survey, respondents to the questionnaire stated overwhelmingly that they learned how to perform their duties in ministry through multiple processes, including being "led by the Spirit," being mentored by a more knowledgeable pastor or leader, participation in a standardized educational program, and being allowed to learn from any mistakes they made while fulfilling their duties. This means that these respondents have also learned the value of participating in multiple modes of ministry development.

Number of Years of Experience

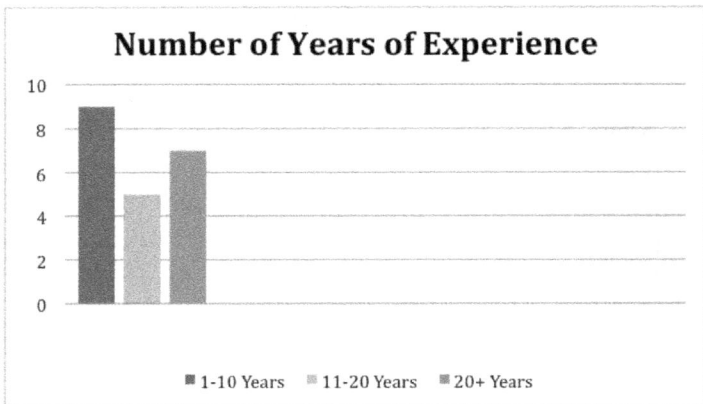

Table 9: Results of Baptist Leadership Questionnaire for Question 6

According to the data acquired, over 70 percent of respondents had participated in a standardized educational program through a Bible-based institute in addition to attending at least one year of college. More specifically, 52 percent had attended and completed a college or Bible college program. Sixty-two percent had completed at least a certificate program. Forty-three percent said that participation in a college or graduate level educational program adequately prepared them for the ministry duties they perform.

In addition to attending programs through traditional educational institutions, respondents had participated in local educational opportunities. The vast majority of respondents—87 percent—had participated in an intentional church-, district-, or state convention-based training program. Participation in these programs typically leads to relevant certification recognized by the participant's home congregation upon completion.

This type of training is typically accomplished within a conference setting and occurs at least quarterly. The majority of respondents stated that they use what they learn through these trainings on a regular basis.

In addition to participating in traditional and nontraditional educational programs, respondents participated in structured mentoring relationships. The overwhelming majority had participated in an intentional mentoring relationship for at least three years and met with a mentor at least once a week.

Participants' meetings with mentors occurred through personal one-on-one meetings or phone calls, with one-on-one meetings being the preferred option among mentees. The majority of respondents reported that they continue to maintain a relationship with their mentor even after the formal mentoring process has ended. The majority of respondents use what they learn from their mentor on a regular basis. Additionally, at least half of the mentors identified by respondents had an earned college or seminary degree.

The makeup of the research sample was overwhelmingly male, with an average age of fifty-nine. Respondents were typically ordained and had to complete an intentional process of learning new knowledge in order to become ordained.

PHASE 2B: INVESTIGATION

Phase 2B consisted of the investigation of whether or not any national, state, or local Missionary Baptist entity offered a standardized program of theological education within the context of this study. I located one such program through the National Baptist Convention Inc. (NBC) and the Sunday School Publishing Board (SSPB).

The SSPB is the official publisher of the NBC. The NBC is the national Baptist body that the Baptist Convention of the State of Missouri and most local Baptist congregations affiliate with, including the Union and Antioch Baptist Districts. The SSPB serves more than 36,000 churches and offers resources for member churches that "seek to encourage sound curriculum, relevant Bible study material, and spiritual growth and discipleship resources to meet the needs of member congregations."[1]

---

1. Anthony, *Christian Education*, 1.

Within the SSPB, there is the Division of Christian Education Accreditation and Credentials (DCEAC). The purpose of the DCEAC is to provide

> ... direction and oversight to the Christian Leadership Schools (CLS) program, a program of study that supports the National Baptist Convention at all levels, locally and nationally. The DCEAC provides evaluation and accrediting support for courses taught under the covering of the NBC. Likewise, the DCEAC provides and sets the standards for instructors and administrators connected with the CLS program. All instructors and deans are certified through the DCEAC. Likewise, all schools are accredited through the DCEAC. Courses taught through the CLS are designed to benefit Christian educators, pastors and ministers, and individuals who desire to increase their knowledge and proficiency in the work of the Church.[2]

The Christian Education Leadership Program that has been developed by the SSPB incorporates input and expertise from members of the organization's overall leadership, as well as trained academics working within an accredited college. In fact, "the Christian Education ministry of the National Baptist Convention USA, Inc., is a collaborative work of the National Congress of Christian Education, the American Baptist College, and the Division of Christian Education of the Sunday School Publishing Board."[3]

The commitment by the NBC to this program of education is exhibited through the extensive structure it has instituted to ensure collaboration and quality education from the national to the local level. Within that structure, the SSPB holds responsibility for overseeing member congregations' Christian Education Leadership Schools:

> Christian Leadership Schools (CLS) represent a unified effort of the NBC to equip the membership to more effectively minister to the body of Christ. A CLS can take

2. Ibid.
3. Ibid.

place in the local churches, in the districts, or at state and national levels. The aim of the CLS Program is to provide structured training and development activities that will take place at all levels of our Baptist denomination. Its goal is to better prepare individuals to become witnesses in accordance with Acts 1:8—"Ye shall receive power, after that the Holy Ghost is come upon you: and ye shall be witnesses unto me both in Jerusalem, and in all Judea, and in Samaria, and unto the uttermost part of the earth" (KJV).[4]

Oversight of this program by the SSPB includes accrediting leadership schools, certifying instructors to teach, formulating policies and procedures governing Christian Education Leadership Schools, designing and developing curricula for the Christian Education Program, and identifying textbooks to be used. Additional standard procedures and required guidelines are necessary for the accreditation and operation of all Christian Leadership Schools, all of which have been approved by the Division of Christian Education Accreditation and Credentials (DCEAC), including thirteen steps required to obtain school accreditation.

These steps are thoroughly explained in the *Christian Leadership School Policies and Procedures Manual* that all campuses are required to adhere to. A partial list of required steps includes selecting and certifying a campus dean, establishing a clear budget for the school and relevant financial methods to be followed, selecting or creating a series of courses to offer, selecting and certifying all instructors for the school, conducting faculty meetings, developing a program format, and submitting an *Annual Dean's Report*.

Additionally, the SSPB oversees the Certificate of Progress Program (COPP). The COPP is the standard program offered through any CLS affiliated with NBC that seeks to nurture church leadership development through a four-phase certification process. The objectives of the COPP are to "increase biblical knowledge; create an understanding of the Baptist church; provide an

4. Ibid.

educational structure that will develop candidates who are qualified for teaching and leadership positions; provide incentives for the candidate to complete the program; and, produce trained church leaders."[5]

While the COPP seeks to train church leaders for teaching, lay persons who wish to increase their understanding of the biblical text and become more effective disciples of Jesus are encouraged to enroll in the COPP as well. Entrance requirements for the program are similar to those found in multiple regionally accredited college programs.

The course offerings for COPP are divided into four phases. Although there is flexibility in how students complete the program, COPP participants are encouraged to take the courses in a specific order because each phase builds on the previous phase over a five-year period.

Phases and courses are as follows:

> "*Phase I*—Effective Bible Reading, Introduction to the Old Testament, Introduction to the New Testament, Christian Stewardship, Theology and History of Christianity, and Spiritual Formation.

> *Phase II*—The Synoptic Gospels, Baptist Doctrine, The Doctrine of the Holy Spirit, Discovering Your Spiritual Gifts, Writing Techniques I.

> *Phase III*—Survey of John, Survey of Romans, History of Baptists, Christian Evangelism, Writing Techniques II.

> *Phase IV*—Survey of Revelations, Foundations of Christian Ethics, Organizing the Church for Christian Education, The Computer in the Life of the Church, Christianity and Contemporary Issues."[6]

---

5. Ibid.
6. Ibid.

Significance of the COPP Program to This Project

Based on personal interactions and conversations with multiple leaders within the St. Louis Missionary Baptist community, I began the research process assuming there was not a singular program of theological leadership development featuring a high standard of development and implementation available to leaders outside of traditional theological educational institutions' offerings. I was wrong in this assumption.

The instruction offered through the COPP and administered by NBC-affiliated CLS are structured and monitored just as any other reputable program offered by an accredited Bible college or seminary would be.

Additionally, the programs and program personnel are given an initial evaluation in order to become accredited, and they are evaluated on a regular basis in order to maintain their accreditation through NBC. The benefits of this process include consistency in the doctrine and practices used by those teaching future ministry leaders. In fact,

> The process of accrediting a school ensures that certain standards of education and training are met, in terms of what is being taught and who is doing the teaching. Accredited schools can be held at all levels—national, state, district, and local. The procedures for accrediting a school do not vary. The same requirements that must be met by the local church holding an accredited Christian education school must be met at every level. The necessary paperwork is prepared by the dean of the school and submitted to the DCEAC. Since all programs must meet the same requirements, any course taken at any accredited program can be utilized at any level. The required courses can be taken at the local church, the district, the state, or at the National Congress, as long as the program has been accredited by the DCEAC.[7]

Having identified Christian education as a continuing need within member churches, NBC developed a comprehensive plan

7. Ibid.

to address that need. There is a consistent level of preparation required of anyone hoping to serve within a CLS. The expectations of all teachers and administrators within a CLS or COPP are clearly outlined and are consistent throughout every location.

Additionally, anyone who seeks to lead or teach in the program is expected to participate in a set process for gaining knowledge and learning how to share that knowledge. Moreover, there is a regular process for continuing education and evaluation for all leaders of these programs. The NBC's process of Christian education is illustrated by the following diagram.

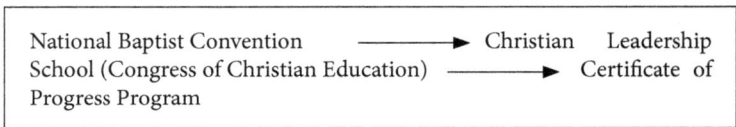

National Baptist Convention ⎯⎯⎯⎯▶ Christian Leadership School (Congress of Christian Education) ⎯⎯⎯⎯▶ Certificate of Progress Program

Diagram 1: Educational Program of the National Baptist Convention

Some of the benefits of this model are that the program offerings were developed by African American leaders who practice their craft in predominantly African American congregations and organizations. Most courses are taught by other African Americans and relate to the experiences of black pastors and leaders. Based on reviews of the course material conducted in comparison to the stated needs and desires of research participants, the material is relevant to their personal experiences and recognizes their unique needs in leading congregations of color.

PHASE 2C: INTERVIEWS

With the understanding that there is a national model for standardized theological education already in place, Phase 2C consisted of interviewing the president of the Missionary Baptist Convention of the State of Missouri (MBCSM) in order to learn how the national model is used on the state level. The president of MBCSM is one of the most powerful and influential Missionary Baptists in the state. This position typically carries with it a corresponding position within the NBC. The president provides leadership to 300 congregations, with 102 of those congregations located in the St. Louis Metropolitan area. The current president has served in his position for nine years and has two years remaining in his term at the time of this writing.

Additionally, the president's views and opinions set the tone for the majority of Missionary Baptist in Missouri. Ultimately, his opinion and actions concerning theological education set the tone for churches located in the St. Louis region. The current president has earned multiple unaccredited degrees and has participated in accredited doctoral-level formation through the Beeson Institute for Advanced Church Leadership at Asbury Seminary.

Interview questions asked of the president sought to understand the views and practices of the State Convention as it relates to the importance of education, how ministers and leaders are taught to perform various ministry functions, the form training programs take, the frequency of training programs, the educational requirements for those who train other pastors and leaders, and how these training programs are evaluated by students.

The president affirmed that the educational program currently in place for the State Convention's member congregations is based solely on the CLS COPP model that exists on the national level. The State Convention uses the accreditation procedures instituted by the SSPB, the processes for identifying and preparing instructors outlined by the SSPB, the curriculum developed and required by the COPP, and also the process already in existence to evaluate both leaders and courses.

In addition to the SSPB program, the MBCSM supports Western Baptist Bible College (WBBC), a Bible college located in Kansas City, Missouri. Western is said to be the first and only Christian institution of higher learning west of the Mississippi River founded exclusively by blacks. The college was founded in 1890. The college's purpose is, first, to meet the demands of ministerial training and, second, to provide education for young people guided by Christian influence. The college boasts campuses in

Kansas City, Topeka, Wichita, Olathe, and Junction City, Kansas, as well as in St. Louis, Missouri.

Western is popular among many pastors and leaders within the St. Louis Missionary Baptist community, partly due to the support of the president of MBCSM. He has developed an extensive plan to rehabilitate many of the buildings on Western's campus. Additionally, several long-tenured pastors and leaders who are active and respected within the State Convention have graduated from Western, received an honorary doctor of divinity, or taught for the college at one of its various campuses. The college had ninety-nine students at the end of its 2014 fiscal year.

Although Western is a duly recognized school within the state of Missouri, one of its continuing challenges has been its lack of accreditation. In the past, Western has claimed accreditation from the Accrediting Commission International, a proven accreditation mill that is not recognized by the Council for Higher Education Accreditation (CHEA), which is the standard-bearer for traditionally recognized accrediting agencies.

One of the reasons that Western is unable to gain accreditation is a lack of recognized credentials among its staff and faculty. In the college's *2014 Annual Report*, the school listed thirty-two staff and faculty members. No degrees were listed for any of them. After conducting an Internet search for the listed faculty and staff, I was able to locate the credentials of only one faculty member who had earned an accredited degree. In addition to not having adequately credentialed faculty and staff, the college does not possess either an endowment or an adequate library. These are two immediate factors that hinder Western from gaining acceptable accreditation.

In spite of these issues, in 2014, Western was accepted as an Affiliate Member of the Association of Biblical Higher Education (ABHE). The ABHE, formerly known as the American Association of Bible Colleges, was organized in 1947 and offers a variety of programs and services to affiliate institutions that help those institutions show evidence of operating as a viable institution of higher learning, such as administration development, instructor continuing education opportunities, and financial management practices. Western's Affiliate Member status does not constitute, imply, or presume ABHE accredited status at present or in the future.

In spite of these accreditation concerns, Western operates as a full college with admission procedures and standards that are similar to other accredited institutions. The college also offers multiple traditional theologically-centered degree programs, including the doctor of ministry. In addition to these degree programs, Western also offers a COPP based on the NBC model, making it similar to the program offered by the MBCSM.

Leadership education options through the MBCSM are illustrated in the following diagram.

Missionary Baptist Convention of the State of Missouri ⟶ Western Baptist Bible College/Congress of Christian Education/Christian Leadership School ⟶ Certificate of Progress Program/Leadership courses/ Degree or certificate program

Diagram 2: Educational Programs on the State Level

Significance of This Information to This Project

Based on the information provided by the president of the MBCSM, it is evident that the State Convention follows the lead of the NBC as it relates to leadership development. The State Convention is diligent in following the pattern and practices developed by the NBC, and it is also diligent in ensuring that member congregations within the State Convention follow those patterns and practices on a regular basis. This process ensures that what pastors and leaders are learning is consistent between the national and state levels.

When this study was begun, I already knew about the existence of Western Baptist Bible College and its programs. I was also familiar with its significance to the Missionary Baptist community in St. Louis due to my personal affiliation with multiple pastors and leaders who participated in classes through the institution.

The continued existence of Western reinforces the fact that the Missionary Baptist Church holds an ongoing interest in addressing ongoing Christian education needs for pastors and leaders.

The concern I have with Western is that the overwhelming majority of staff and faculty do not hold credentials from legitimately accredited educational institutions. I have found anecdotal evidence that the majority of Western staff and faculty are in place due to loyalty to particular leaders within the MBCSM, not because of specific academic qualifications. I do, however, appreciate the fact that Western has gained Affiliate Member status with ABHE and is now operating within an educational fellowship that requires a specific set of criteria and a set framework in order to participate.

PHASE 2D: MODERATOR INTERVIEWS

Moderator Interviews

The final portion of this process involved conducting one-on-one interviews with the current moderators of two Baptist districts where research was conducted: the Union and Antioch Baptist Districts. These two moderators were chosen because they were the only moderators who accepted my invitation to participate in the interview process. The purpose of conducting these interviews was to gain specific insight into how each district viewed theological education and whether either district had adopted a policy or practice related to theological education and training.

I initiated these two interviews with much anticipation because each moderator has vastly different personal experiences related to participation in traditional theological education. The moderator for the Union District has not completed an accredited degree program, while the moderator for the Antioch District has earned an accredited master of divinity, doctor of ministry, and juris doctorate. In spite of the differences in their levels of formal education, both moderators believe that regular participation in some type of education and training program is one key to the success of congregational leaders.

The moderator of the Union District, who has served in his position for three years, has instituted a new training program within the last year that seeks to provide monthly training opportunities to pastors, leaders, and laity within the district's churches. The initiative is called the Christian Leadership School and has as its motto "to train and nurture all in Christian education."

The purpose of the CLS is to "ground attendees in the Word of God and assist them in fulfilling the Great Commission."[8] The program is administered by the moderator with help from designated people within the district. The cost to attendees is $10 per session.

In addition to the CLS, the Union District participates in a second training program through the Sunday School Publishing Board. The courses and format of these courses were developed by the National Congress of Christian Education (CCE) of the SSPB. Instructors who teach through the Union District must be certified to teach through the SSPB. The SSPB program and requirements will be fully explained shortly.

The Antioch District has had an intentional two-fold leadership training program in place for several years. The training component that requires a fee has been in existence since 1949, while the free component has been in place since 2013.

The programs for both districts are based on the COPP instituted by the NBC. The programs are accredited by the SSPB and follow the same requirements as those for the COPP instituted by the MBCSM and Western Baptist Bible College. The leadership programs available in the Antioch and Union Districts is illustrated in the following diagram:

8 Donald Ray McNeal (pastor and district moderator) in discussion with the author, June 2013.

District Department/Program/Congress of Christian Education/Christian Leadership School ⟶ Certificate of Progress Program/Leadership courses/Certificate program ⟶ Local Congregation

Diagram 3: Educational Programs on the Congregational Level

Significance of This Information to This Project

Based on the information provided by the moderators of the two districts, it is evident that multiple local districts follow the lead of the NBC and MBCSM as it relates to leadership development. Several districts are diligent in following the pattern and practices that have been developed by the NBC and emulated by the MBCSM, and these local districts are also diligent in ensuring that member congregations within the districts follow those patterns and practices on a regular basis. This process ensures that what pastors and leaders are learning is consistent from the national level to the state level.

What the Data from Phase 2 Shows

From the data collected through Phase 2, I learned that there is a standardized program of theological and leadership education that pastors and leaders affiliated with the National Baptist Convention, the Missionary Baptist State Convention of Missouri, or one of its affiliate districts—including the Union and Antioch Districts—are strongly encouraged to participate in. This program has the potential to reach pastors and leaders within at least 102 churches within the St. Louis metropolitan region.

This program of learning has been intentionally developed and has undergone multiple revisions and changes in order to ensure program quality, adequate program administration, and accountability. When I began this project, I was unaware of the depth of work that had been committed to this program and the consistency present from the national to local levels and was pleasantly surprised with the considerable lengths to which those involved with the development and administration of the program have gone to ensure program quality and a level of consistency.

Data collected also shows that pastors and leaders affiliated with the above-mentioned conventions and districts—as well as with districts that did not participate in this research project— have ample opportunity to participate in some type of leadership development program on at least a monthly basis. Based on the interviews conducted with the president of the MBCSM and moderators of the two districts, it is evident that great emphasis is placed on as many members as possible within local congregations participating in these programs. This includes laity who have no desire to teach within a ministry setting or any discernible call to ministry involvement.

Data also revealed that multiple leaders on the state and lo-cal level have participated in traditional accredited theological education programs. These leaders have a continuing appreciation for such programs. This appreciation drives these leaders to en-courage—and sometimes require—others to participate in simi-lar programs when they are able. If others are unable to acquire traditional theological education, these leaders encourage them to participate in the programs currently offered through national, state, and local entities.

An added benefit of having buy-in from leaders who have participated in traditional theological education programs is that such leaders are uniquely qualified, based on their prior learning opportunities, to evaluate the training programs offered through NBC, MBCSM, and local districts and to provide much-needed assessment skills.

Concerns Raised by the Data

Although I learned encouraging information about the educa-tional programs offered to local African American Baptist pastors and leaders, the data also raised concerns. The first concern is for pastors and leaders who are not affiliated with any of the organizations highlighted in this chapter. Although the MBCSM claims at least 102 member congregations from the St. Louis metropolitan area, there are at least fifty-two independent African American Baptist congregations that do not affiliate with the MBCSM. What educational opportunities are available to these congregations and leaders?

A second concern is that although participation in CLCs and COPPs are strongly encouraged, no one can make a pastor or leader attend any of the trainings. I was unable to acquire data on exact numbers of how many pastors and leaders attended the available trainings or how many opted not to attend. This information would have proven valuable in trying to determine the percentage of pastors and leaders that participated versus those who chose not to participate.

A third concern raised by the data is the question of how much overlap in teaching is occurring from the local to the national level. If the program options are being offered on a regular basis on the local, state, and national levels, learners may experience information overload due to the frequency at which courses are offered. Additionally, I question whether each course offering is providing new information to the learner, or whether courses may be redundant.

A fourth concern raised by the data relates to one specific desire voiced by the research participants about preferred learning opportunities. Research participants in Phase 1 stated that they valued standardized educational programs, ongoing professional development opportunities, and participation in mentoring relationships. The first two items are clearly covered through the multiple programs identified in this research. The desire for regular mentoring relationships has not been addressed. If pastors or leaders participate in a pastors and/or ministers union or fellowship, they have regular opportunities to engage in mentoring relationships with other pastors and leaders. If they do not participate in such a group, they may not have mentoring opportunities outside of what their own pastor has time to facilitate.

A fifth concern deals with the lack of diversity in what program participants may learn through the CLS and COPP. There is great value in the fact that these programs are geared specifically to pastors and leaders who serve within Missionary Baptist congregations. They ensure that learners interact with material and ideas that hold great relevance to their immediate community.

The concern is that learners' interaction with material that may challenge their beliefs or understanding of certain doctrines or practices may be limited. Through these programs, learners may never interact with material or authors who hold different views than their own, which could mean that their faith and theological position on certain issues may never be fully developed through the process of interacting with dissenting viewpoints.

A sixth concern deals with the qualifications of the people who lead and teach within the CLS and COPP. The NBC has done an admirable job of developing a streamlined process for identifying and educating the people who lead and administer the CLS and COPP. I understands that in order to be an administrator or instructor in any of these programs, you must participate in multiple courses and adhere to multiple rules.

Nevertheless, I can imagine circumstances where an administrator or teacher is allowed to participate based solely on their connection to an influential national, state, or local leader who wants to put them into a position of influence or authority. I was unable to determine whether there is a safeguard within the accreditation process for the SSPB that seeks to deter this type of situation from occurring.

The final concern raised by the data was the question of what is next for learners after completing the COPP. What other continuing education opportunities can pastors and leaders look forward to? Since each congregation is autonomous and participates with the local, state, and national bodies on a voluntary basis, no single entity is able to require pastors and leaders to participate in any program. I learned that after the completing the COPP, students are able to continue their studies through three additional certification processes that use the COPP as the foundation.

Although there are more levels of certification available, is this overall process adequate to meet student needs?

Further concerns were raised as a result of the accumulated data. These concerns do not relate to the CLS or COPP but instead relate to the educational opportunities made available by Western Baptist Bible College, the school that is closely affiliated with the MBCSM. I remain concerned about the influence Western may have on local pastors and leaders.

Western lacks the requisite number of staff and faculty who hold credentials from accredited institutions in order to teach on the college or seminary level. Through multiple conversations with faculty members and people affiliated with the institution, I have ascertained that there are essentially four ways that people become instructors for Western.

First, a prominent student will be invited to become a faculty member after earning ministry degrees from Western. Second, pastors and leaders of congregations that have made substantial monetary contributions to the institution are asked to become instructors. Third, when a prominent pastor or leader is conferred an honorary doctor of divinity from the institution, they will likely be invited to become an instructor. Fourth, pastors and leaders who have provided political and social support for certain people who have campaigned for local, state, and national ministry positions within the Missionary Baptist community will often be rewarded with opportunities to teach at Western. None of these practices ensure that qualified instructors are in place.

I understand that academic degrees do not guarantee a capable instructor. I also acknowledge that those who may not have earned a traditional academic degree can still make valuable contributions within an academic setting. My concern is that Western presents itself as an institution that provides students with a high-quality education, but I wonder if this is possible, considering the lack of credentialed staff and faculty as well as the school's limited resources.

Chapter Seven

Opportunities for the Future

THIS STUDY SOUGHT TO understand several things. It sought to understand the attitudes that are held by Missionary Baptist pastors and leaders in St. Louis concerning traditionally accredited educational programs. It sought to discover the most frequent ways that Missionary Baptist pastors and leaders participated in ministry training. It also sought to discover the ways that pastors and leaders preferred to engage in theological and leadership training.

As a result of this research, insight was gained into the views Missionary Baptist pastors and leaders hold towards education and the educational programs they most frequently participate in. This insight has led me to form four conclusions specific to the educational needs of Missionary Baptist pastors and leaders in St. Louis, as well as a model to address those needs.

CONCLUSION 1: TRADITIONAL PROGRAMS DO NOT ADDRESS SPECIFIC NEEDS IDENTIFIED BY AFRICAN AMERICAN STUDENTS

From the data collected through Phase 1 of this project, I learned that pastors and leaders hold a deep desire to learn new, relevant information and apply that information to their regular ministry practices. As I discovered through participant comments, it is evident that these pastors and leaders believe they learn and retain new information best when they are involved in an educational process that recognizes their unique experiences as African American ministry leaders who are trying to meet the needs of other African Americans. These types of programs typically occur through organizations that are somehow affiliated with leaders' home church, local church district, state convention, or national convention.

Additionally, pastors and leaders want to participate in programs that help them to become more effective preachers and teachers with the requisite skills to regularly address the spiritual and social needs of their congregation members. These training opportunities do not have to occur only within a classroom setting.

The data shows that ministry leaders learn many necessary skills through participating in a mentoring relationship with a person who has more relevant experience and who can regularly answer their questions and provide encouragement and ideas that they can implement in their own ministry settings. This finding presents an opportunity to modify existing educational programs—or create new ones—that take these points into account.

CONCLUSION 2: REFLECTION IS NEEDED IN ORDER TO TAKE PROPER ACTION

Based on the research conducted, formal modes of education for ministry preparation in African American Baptist churches are not the standard. In the black church tradition, leadership preparation can occur through multiple formats, the most important being an internal pulling and urging towards the ministry that comes directly from God. This pulling, or calling, is evidenced through a prospective leader's ability to communicate God's love and faithfulness to God's children through the act of preaching and teaching on a regular basis.

There is an expectation that this ability to preach and teach will improve over time due to the prospective leader's faithfulness to their call to ministry and regular exercise of that gift. With this in mind, there is an opportunity for educational institutions to consider developing new programs that take this tradition of not setting expectations for participation in a standardized educational process into account, as well as rethink their strategies for marketing their programs to Missionary Baptist pastors and leaders.

CONCLUSION 3: THREE PARAMETERS MUST BE TAKEN INTO ACCOUNT WHEN ATTEMPTING TO ADDRESS THE EDUCATIONAL NEEDS OF AFRICAN AMERICAN STUDENTS

This research revealed that a program exists through the Sunday School Publishing Board of the National Baptist Convention that meets the stated needs and desires of African American Baptist pastors and leaders. This program, which was developed by black pastors and leaders specifically for black pastors and leaders, keeps the African American experience as its core principle, maintains a high level of consistency in requirements for program administrators as well as teachers and educational materials, and provides students with opportunities to contribute to program improvement through evaluations. All of these educational aims are achieved while maintaining a reasonable level of economic affordability.

Participants in this program are not deterred by the fact that this program issues certificates that are only endorsed by a state or national Baptist entity and thus do not count as academic credit earned towards a degree pursued through a traditionally accredited educational program.

Participants are willing to earn the certificates because within the learning process, they are being prepared to meet the needs of their current congregations while simultaneously participating in opportunities to build camaraderie with other pastors and leaders and also pursue mentoring relationships. To these pastors and leaders, these opportunities are more important than obtaining an accredited degree.

CONCLUSION 4: PARTICIPATION IN A NEW PROCESS THAT SEEKS TO FILL THE NEEDS OF AFRICAN AMERICAN BAPTIST PASTORS AND LEADERS

There is a gap between the desired means of obtaining theological and leadership education as stated by African American Baptist leaders and the current educational offerings available through accredited institutions of higher learning in St. Louis. Although accreditation is a secondary concern for many Baptist pastors and leaders, this does not mean that traditional universities and seminaries should give up on clarifying the need for and benefits of accreditation. Many students do not understand the value of accreditation because it has never been explained to them or they have not been required to obtain an accredited education for employment.

Awareness of this gap as it relates the thinking about accreditation—and subsequent attempts to bridge it—can prove beneficial to traditional seminaries and universities because better awareness and continued attempts to bridge this gap may lead to increasingly effective programs of education for black students, as well as an opportunity to reach an untapped market for students in the St. Louis area. This would also be beneficial to potential students because new learning opportunities might be made available to them that address their stated needs while also allowing them to continue and complete their education through an accredited institution.

FINAL RECOMMENDATIONS: INCORPORATE SPECIFIC PARAMETERS WHEN ATTEMPTING TO ADDRESS EDUCATIONAL NEEDS OF AFRICAN AMERICAN BAPTIST PASTORS AND LEADERS

In order for traditional universities and seminaries to improve and expand educational opportunities to African American Baptist pastors, educational institutions and ministry leaders will need to engage in a four-pronged conversation that may make both parties uncomfortable. This will require educational institutions to participate in such conversations from a position of a learner seeking to gain and understand new information. African American Baptist leaders and pastors will likewise need to set aside their distrust towards traditional educational institutions in order to be open to any new opportunities for learning that may be presented.

RECOMMENDATION 1: INCORPORATE NEW LANGUAGE THAT SPEAKS TO THE NEEDS OF AFRICAN AMERICAN BAPTIST PASTORS AND LEADERS

African American Baptist pastors and leaders can work towards changing the pervasive internal narrative that says traditional learning programs are not necessary. This task will not be simple or instantaneous. It will have to incorporate multiple long-term strategies that address local, state, and national prejudices that have been held for decades. I have not found a comprehensive approach to accomplishing this task, but I was able to find an extensive framework to consider as a foundation for formulating a plan to accomplish this goal.

The challenges that will need to be faced in order for this internal change to occur were best summarized by Dr. Johnson when he said that we have to

> ... destroy myths about seminary, find associational, state, and national leaders who promote theological education, create trusts and scholarships, create tutorial and

> learning centers in our local church, tackle the literacy problem within our local church and its surrounding communities, invest more of our church budget into Christian Education and educational ministries, be willing to assist associate clergy in their pursuit of academic studies, redevelop ordination catechism curriculum, have more pastors promote seminary from their church, have association, state, and nation-wide seminary sign-up events, and partner with undergraduate religion programs to shorten the completion time of a Master of Divinity.[1]

Clearly, this task will not be simple, but it can begin with African American Baptist pastors and leaders who have attended and completed traditional educational programs and are not afraid to defend their experiences within those programs.

Conversely, traditional seminaries and universities have the opportunity to evaluate the core principles of their program offerings and to take steps to make those programs more accessible to potential students whose backgrounds do not include traditional higher-level learning experiences. This would begin with intentional changes to the language used within classrooms. Instructors and administrators would need to "adjust their vocabulary by making the complexity and difficulty of the style . . . agree with the level of the target audience. Change illustrations in order to adopt the images and figures to ones [that are] within the experience and traditions of the target audience. Recast content to reflect [the] worldview[s] of those [they are] intending to reach. Adjust to the learning styles of those [they are] intending to reach."[2]

I realize that this is not the practice of most traditional institutions of higher learning. I also recognize that the expectation is that learners will make these types of adjustments in order to raise their intellectual abilities to certain levels and to gain specified sets of knowledge. This suggestion is not an indication that I believe institutions should "dumb down" their material. Instead, I

---

1. Johnson, "Theological Pathways," 103–104

2. Ward, *Effective Learning*, 106.

suggest that institutions modify how material is presented in order for students to better to grasp the material and its meanings via vocabulary and information that is relevant to their experiences.

RECOMMENDATION 2: MAKE NEW FACULTY AND ADMINISTRATIVE HIRES

One way to address African American Baptist's long-held distrust is for traditional educational institutions to hire faculty and administration that share some of the same cultural experiences as their future students. Dr. Ward provides a set of suggestions for how this can be accomplished. He states that any instructor or administrator should be "Knowledgeable in the subject matter and a successful practitioner of his subject or skill; Enthusiastic about the subject and about teaching it; Understanding about people; Creative in thinking about teaching methods and willing to experiment and innovate to meet changing needs and interests; More concerned with the development of the individual than with just a presentation of facts; and respected in the community or occupation group."[3] Ultimately, this would mean that instructors who originate from the African American Baptist community and have completed accredited degree programs would be the best candidates to teach this potential group of students.

RECOMMENDATION 3: INCORPORATE A PHILOSOPHY OF CURRICULUM DEVELOPMENT THAT SEEKS TO MEET THE SPECIFIC NEEDS OF AFRICAN AMERICAN BAPTIST STUDENTS

Traditional educational institutions can develop new programs designed specifically to meet the needs of African American Baptist pastors and leaders as well as nontraditional adult learners— an idea previously suggested by Dr. Dixon. He has stated, "White theological schools can meet the Black challenge by establishing

3. Ibid., 112.

special study programs to meet the educational needs of. . . ministers and other religious leaders. Most of these religious leaders do not hold college or seminary degrees. Some have not even earned high school diplomas. Special study programs to upgrade the performance of these religious leaders would tap a mighty resource for good, for God."[4]

In order for this change to occur successfully, educational institutions can begin conversations with the Baptist districts and the Baptist State Conventions that have an established presence and influence in their regions. Those conversations can lead a willing institution to form a partnership with the State Conventions in order to develop undergraduate degree completion programs that use the COPP curriculum as their foundation.

These potential programs could use Problem-Based Learning (PBL) as their foundation. PBL, sometimes called Issues-Based Curriculum, is a student-centered way of teaching in which students learn about a subject through the process of identifying a problem and how to correct that problem. The goal of having students participate in this type of learning process is to help them develop flexible knowledge, effective problem-solving skills, self-directed learning, effective collaboration skills, and motivation to solve a problem that would help improve something they are involved in. Once these problem-solving skills have been developed, they can be used for the remainder of students' lives.

This educational process could begin with students identifying what they already know about a particular subject, what they need to know in order to solve the particular problem currently faced, and where they can access the necessary information to bring resolution to the problem. The instructor helps facilitate the learning process by strategically supporting, guiding, and monitoring the learners—typically six to ten (6–10) students—and their efforts to solve the problem.

The main challenge for implementing this type of learning process will be found in how instructors can best support the learning process for each student:

4. Dixon, will white theol schools meet the black challenge?

In order to instill a project based learning environment into a classroom, the teacher must revolve his or her teaching style around five main criteria. Centrality, driving question, constructive investigations, autonomy, and realism. The first being centrality, the projects are the curriculum in this case so everything the student needs to learn should be centered on the project that he or she is working on. The second criterion that a teacher must meet is that there must be a driving question that the student must answer through completing the project. This question is the most important aspect to a successful project based learning environment because it is what motivates the student to learn as well as gives the student an idea of what knowledge is expected to be learned from the project. Also the question cannot have a predetermined outcome, it should require the student to use prior knowledge to come up with a conclusion; however, the project should not be able to be put together based solely on prior knowledge. The other criteria are constructive investigations, autonomy, and realism, all of these are important for the student because it helps pull the student into the project and capture the attention as well as allows for the student to make connections to real world situations. This is more beneficial than a test because the students have to make these connections on their own and gather information that interests them instead of just memorizing facts for a test.[5]

I think this learning model would be more beneficial to the development of African American Baptist pastors and leaders than a traditional educational process because it is based on the idea of trying to solve relevant problems, takes into account what the student already knows, frames the relationship between instructor and student as being based in teamwork, intentionally supports a cohort-based learning model that would enable students to mentor each other based on their personal level of knowledge and experience, and does not require students to become weighed down

---

5. Krajeik et al., "Collaborative Model," 483–97.

with learning information that they do not consider relevant to their particular ministry context.

The PBL model can be used to develop not only undergraduate programs that address the needs and challenges of African American Baptist pastors and leaders as well as other nontraditional students in St. Louis, it could also be used to develop graduate and doctoral-level programs that are based more on research and problem-solving than on memorization of a certain set of facts.

Programs that can be considered are the master of divinity with a concentration in ministry leadership, or doctor of ministry with a concentration in black church leadership, or doctor of professional studies with an emphasis in black church studies, or a doctor of intercultural studies with an emphasis in black church studies. All of these degree titles and areas of emphasis are listed as acceptable degree designations by the Association of Theological Schools.

FOR FURTHER STUDY

Several intriguing questions arose from this project that may call for further study. A small sampling of areas for future research that, if studied in-depth, could provide beneficial ideas for the continued development of African American Baptist pastors and leaders in St. Louis are as follows:

- A comparative study of the information learned through courses and programs such as the COPP offered by the NBC, MBCSM, and local Baptist districts versus information learned through accredited academic institutions

- A comparative study of the academic and practical qualifications of instructors who teach within the COPP and the corresponding qualifications of those who teach at accredited academic institutions

- A study to understand if and how pastors and leaders grow spiritually and academically before and after participation in the COPP

- A study to understand if and how pastors and leaders grow spiritually and academically before and after participation in an accredited program

- A study to understand the outreach practices and effectiveness of congregations led by pastors and leaders who only participate in the COPP in comparison to congregations led by pastors and leaders with degrees from traditionally accredited institutions

- A study to understand and evaluate the administrative practices and effectiveness of pastors and leaders who have only participated in the COPP in comparison to pastors and leaders who have participated in traditionally accredited programs

- A study that compares the preaching practices and effectiveness of pastors and leaders who have only participated in the COPP versus the corresponding practices and effectiveness of pastors who have participated in traditionally accredited programs

- A comparative study to understand the beliefs and practices related to women in ministry held by pastors and leaders who have only participated in the COPP versus the corresponding beliefs and practices employed by pastors and leaders who participated in traditionally accredited degree programs

Conclusion

THE GUIDING RESEARCH QUESTION for this project was "Based on the unique needs of African American Baptist pastors and leaders, what is the most effective process to provide them with ministry development training in order for them to become more effective leaders in their particular contexts?" The findings of this project revealed that the most effective process for training African American Baptist pastors and leaders incorporates the felt needs of pastors and leaders and also seeks their opinions on how to meet those needs.

The most effective training programs acknowledge the distrust held by African American pastors and leaders towards what they consider traditional white theological educational processes that historically have not given blacks an adequate voice in defining and shaping that process. These programs recognize the long-held differences between how whites and blacks have traditionally learned ministry leadership skills and hold those varying experiences as equally beneficial.

These programs are also affiliated with organizations that have a regular presence and relationship with black churches, offer learning experiences through multiple formats, and are taught by instructors who share similar life experiences as the pastors and leaders being taught.

This project has shown that there are opportunities for traditional seminaries and universities to help meet the needs of African American Baptist pastors and leaders through the development of programs that take each of these points into account and create learning opportunities that make potential learners feel welcome and accepted as brothers and sisters in Christ who bring value and experience that can inspire not only other students, but their instructors as well. I pray that this book serves as a catalyst for these types of changes.

Bibliography

Anthony, Judith Logan. "Christian Leadership Schools." *Sunday School Publishing Board*. Accessed April 15, 2013. https://www.sspbnbc.com/divisions/christian-education/christian-leadership-schools/.

Berger, Jennifer Garvey. *Changing on the Job: Developing Leaders for a Complex World*. Stanford: Stanford University Press, 2012.

Briggs, David. "Seminary Debt Rising: Clergy Postpone Starting Families, Face Bankruptcy." *Huffington Post*, August 27, 2012. http://www.huffingtonpost.com/david-briggs/seminary-debt-rising-clergy-postpone-starting-families-face-bankruptcy_b_1821349.html.

Borden, Paul D. *Direct Hit—Aiming Real Leaders at the Mission Field*. Nashville: Abingdon, 2006.

Bradley, Anthony B. *Aliens in the Promised Land: Why Minority Leadership Is Overlooked in White Christian Churches and Institutions*. Phillipsburg, NJ: Presbyterian & Reformed, 2013.

Carroll, Jackson W. "How Do Pastors Practice Leadership?" *Pulpit and Pew: Research on Pastoral Leadership* report, Duke Divinity School, 2000. http://pulpitandpew.org/how-do-pastors-practice-leadership.

City of St. Louis. "A Brief History of the City of St. Louis." *StLouis-MO.gov*. 2016. https://www.stlouis-mo.gov/visit-play/stlouis-history.cfm.

Colvin, Jawanza Karriem. "An Examination of the Professional Development of African American Baptist Pastors: A Comparative Case Study." PhD diss., Columbia University, 2012.

Costen, James H. "Black Theological Education: Its Context, Content, and Conduct." *Journal of the Interdenominational Theological Center* 12 (1984–1985) 1–8.

DeVeaux, Bishop William P. "Prophetic Ministry: The Black Church & Theological Education." *Resources for American Christianity*. September 3, 2001. http://www.resourcingchristianity.org/research-article/prophetic-ministry-the-black-church-theological-education.

Dib, Claudio Zaki. "Formal, Non-Formal and Informal Education: Concepts/Applicability." In *Cooperative Networks in Physics Education: Conference*

Proceedings 173, edited by Jorge Barojas, 300–315. New York: American Institute of Physics, 1988. http://techne-dib.com.br/downloads/6.pdf.

Dixon, Norman R. "Will White Theological Schools Meet the Black Challenge?" *Perspective Magazine*, spring 1972.

Etindi, Diana. "Training Ministers from a Black Church Perspective." PhD diss., Anderson University, 2011.

Farley, Edward. *Theologia: The Fragmentation and Unity of Theological Education*. Eugene: Wipf & Stock, 2001.

Fuder, John. *A Heart for the City: Effective Ministries to the Urban Community*. Chicago: Moody, 2005.

Godfrey, J. Michael. "The Role of Mentoring in the Developmental Experiences of Baptist Pastors in Texas: A Case Study." PhD diss., Baylor University, 2005.

Hinton, Mary. *The Commercial Church: Black Churches and the New Religious Marketplace in America*. New York: Rowman & Littlefield, 2011.

Jinkins, Michael, and Deborah Bradshaw Jinkins. *The Character of Leadership: Political Realism and Public Virtue in Nonprofit Organizations*. San Francisco: Jossey-Bass, 1998.

Jackson, Clarence Eugene. "Church Listings." *Black Church St. Louis*. Accessed May 15, 2013. http://blackchurchstlouis.org/?page_id=4.

Johnson, LaMont J., Sr. "Theological Pathways: The Road to Theological Education in the Black Baptist Church." PhD diss., Drew University, 2012.

Kemp, Stephen. "Church-Based Theological Education." *Antioch School of Church Planting and Leadership Development*. July 30, 2013. http://blog.antiochschool.edu/updates/sneak-peek-church-based-theological-education/.

Krajeik, Joseph, Phyllis C. Blummenfeld, Ronald W. Marx, and Elliot Soloway. "Collaborative Model for Helping Middle Grade Science Teachers Learn Project-Based Instruction." *Chicago Journals* 94 (1994) 483–97.

Laser, Rachel, et al. "Beyond the God Gap: A New Roadmap for Reaching Religious Americans on Public Policy Issues." *Public Religion Research*. June 2010. http://publicreligion.org/site/wp-content/uploads/2011/06/Beyond-the-God-Gap-Religion-Cultural-Issues-Report.pdf.

Mamiya, Larry. "River of Struggle, River of Freedom: Trends among Black Churches and Black Pastoral Leadership." *Pulpit and Pew: Research on Pastoral Leadership* report. Durham, NC: Duke Divinity School, 2006. http://pulpitandpew.org/sites/all/themes/pulpitandpew/files/DUP&PBlackTrendsWEBfinal!.pdf.

Newsome-Camara, Imani-Sheilia. "An Historical and Critical Analysis of Leadership Education of African American Protestant Clergy." PhD diss., Boston University, 2012.

Nguyen, Nghia Van. "Leadership Skills Development in Theological Seminary: Crucial Factors in Creating Effective Local Church Leadership." PhD diss., Pepperdine University, 2008.

Reed, Jeff. "Church-Based Theological Education: Creating a New Paradigm." *New Paradigms for the Post-Modern Church*. October 17, 1992. https://www.bild.org/download/paradigmPapers/1_Creating%20a%20New%20Paradigm.pdf.

Rooks, Charles Shelby. "Crisis in Church Negro Leadership." *Theology Today* 22 (October 1965) 323–35.

"Theological Education and the Black Church." *The Christian Century*, February 12, 1969.

———. "Vision, Reality and Challenge: Black Americans and North American Theological Education, 1959–83." *Theological Education* 20 (1983) 37–52.

Still, Leatha Camille. "A Model for Mentoring Clergy for the Work of Ministry: A How-to Manual for Pastors and Mentors in Omega Baptist Church." PhD diss., United Theological Seminary, 2011.

Turner, William C. *Discipleship for African American Christians: A Journey through the Church Covenant*. Valley Forge, PA: Judson, 2002.

Ward, Ted. *Effective Learning in Non-Formal Education*. East Lansing, MI: Michigan State University Press, 1974.

———. *Programmed Instruction for Theological Education by Extension*. Holt, MI: Michigan State University and the Committee to Assist Missionary Education Overseas, 1970.